BRIDGE WALKER

Dear Anne,

Thank you for "walking" the bridge with me all these years.

Best,
Denise

BRIDGE WALKER

By Denise Gray Meehan

Ponquogue Press
Hampton Bays, L.I., N.Y.
2016

Bridge Walker Copyright © 2016 by Denise Gray Meehan

All rights reserved. No part of this publication may be reproduced, distributed, or transmitted in any form or by any means, including photocopying, recording, or other electronic or mechanical methods, without the prior written permission of the publisher, except in the case of brief quotations embodied in critical reviews and certain other non-commercial uses permitted by copyright law.

Ponquogue Press
Hampton Bays, L.I., N.Y.

Photography by Terry Meehan. Design by Mary O'Brien. Editing by Lynn DiGiacomo

Printed in the United States of America

1. Memoir. 2. Long Island 3. Hamptons

First Printing: September 2016

2 4 6 8 10 9 7 5 3 1

ISBN 978-0-578-18511-8

Acknowledgements

Thank you to my Wednesday Writers at Rogers Memorial Library in Southampton. They have figuratively walked the Bridge with me for the past several years. Special thanks to Carla Riccio, our gentle mentor, who made us feel like writers. But without Mary O'Brien, who handled the technical business of self-publishing, and Lynn DiGiacomo's in-depth editing, Bridge Walker would still be just documents on my computer or loose papers filed in decorative folders.

Dedication

For my husband, Terry, who created a writing room for me complete with my first laptop.

The Warm Up

My life didn't turn out the way I thought it would. I never expected to be a working mother with latch key kids, to be a fallen away Catholic, to be a Hester Prynne, to be divorced in my 40s, to find love later in life, to have a step family. I imagined a duplicate of my stay-at-home mother's life in a large Dutch Colonial with bookcases on either side of the fireplace, with a brood and a mild disdain for the country clubs I would belong to. Instead these seventy years have been messier, richer and sweeter than what I could have conjured up while perusing *Bride Magazine* and sipping tea in my college dorm in the 60s.

I never expected to be a walker instead of a runner. The last time I ran was on the 4th of July, 1999 in a 5K race in Southampton. It was blistering hot, without a breath of air. I swore if I survived I would never run again. It's not that I was a serious runner—just a woman who wanted to get her aerobic exercise over as quickly as possible. Making the transition to walking felt like a demotion.

I never expected a span of concrete to become a fixture in my daily routine, to be my muse as well as my exercise. Once I step onto the Ponquogue Bridge, I close my brain and open my senses and observe: I see road work and it makes me think of plastic surgery; piping plovers, an endangered species, connect me to being a letter writer; surfers in stages of undress suggest a piece on public nakedness.

I never expected to write a memoir, but when I started to use my time on that pavement to notice the wonders around me, *Bridge Walker* began.

The bridge has five green rectangular plaques spaced alongside the pedestrian walkway. Spans 5, 10, 15, 20, 25. I have arranged the essays in mostly chronological order spanning my life from 7 to 70.

I always expected a great life, just not this one.
Come on. Walk with me.

The Walker

Inhaling the sweetness of the privet hedge in bloom at the end of my driveway, I turn onto the road towards the Ponquogue Bridge. There's a strong wind from the north today. I ignore the fact that I'll be walking against it for the mile and a half return lap.

Back in the 70s the Ponquogue Bridge used to be my running route when it was a rickety drawbridge. You could feel it shake when a car rumbled by, and there were spaces large enough to spy a school of snappers.

I understood the necessity of a replacement for the 84-year-old bridge, but I was sad to see it go. It not only connected the mainland to the barrier beach, it linked me to my past. I was seven the first time I crossed it with my family in our blue Buick Roadmaster in the 1950s. My sisters and I leaned out of the cranked down windows and welcomed the cool salty air rippling through our hair.

So I was happy to see that when the new bridge was finished, sections of the old one survived. The body of the wooden construction was removed, but part of its old self, like a right and left arm, remained on either side of the channel as fishing piers.

I dubbed the new, sleek concrete bridge "Verrazano Junior." Some friends and I ran across it before it officially opened in 1986. We decided that its panoramic views of Shinnecock Bay and beyond more than compensated for its lack of character. Every time I travel this space it confirms, "This is why I live here."

At the top of the span, I see surfers with seal-like bodies cutting through a part in the grasses to join friends saddled to waves. Scuba divers slip from a floating dock into the waters beneath the bridge's belly, its cement legs splayed like a prehistoric creature.

It's low tide. Clammers, looking like miniatures in the charcoal mud flats, share the space with snowy white egrets. The sea and sky seem to blend into one cloth as scalloped waves ruffle along the shore in a syncopated song.

People on the bridge are friendly--offering nods, "top of the morning" and comments on the weather. There are regulars depending on the time of day. In the summer teens on their bikes with bogie boards under their arms struggle uphill and fly down the other side.

Span 5

This steep incline and descent are a favorite of serious cyclists and runners as well.

A young woman with long dark hair pulled neatly into a ponytail passes me breathing hard. She is wired. A white cord runs from her ear to the top of her tank top. Long legs pump from below her runner's shorts. Instinctively, I start to run. When I was new to jogging, I used to alternate running a hundred steps then walking until I could switch gears and maintain a steady pace. At one hundred steps, I stop. I realize I am chasing my former self. But I am not that woman anymore.

It took me a while to accept and eventually embrace walking as a substitute for running. Instead of headphones blasting adrenalin, I try to empty my brain and focus on the moment, absorbing the details around me. But today I am aware of my freckled, wrinkled hands and my once long hair now short and curled by the humid air.

Stepping off the curb heading home I see a shell that has been dropped by a seagull more than once. Despite the fact that it's missing pieces, I know it as a conch shell, the Buddhist bugle. As I reach the red roofed Coast Guard Station at the base of the bridge, reveille trumpets a new day.

Memories of Nassau Road

It feels like kids' day on the bridge this morning. A group of pre-teen boys wearing bike helmets and orange vests play follow the leader across the bridge. Four birds with yellow beaks chatter away, "Catch me if you can." Dipping and diving like aerial artists, they bank to one side flashing white bellies. An osprey chick watches from his nest.

When I was a child in the 1950s, "Go outside and play" seemed to be every mother's mandate. I was five when we moved from Elmhurst to 67 Nassau Road in Great Neck with my three younger sisters and one on the way. Initially our recreation was confined to a square backyard and a swing set with two rings and a two-seated glider we rode like horses and pretended to be Annie Oakley.

I don't know how my sister Laura did it. One day instead of holding the rings with her hands and swinging, she managed to insert her legs and hang upside down like a gymnast. Very impressive, but she couldn't free her legs and began to panic as the blood rushed to her head. It seemed like a long time to us before our mother acknowledged our screams and rescued her.

On starless August nights when sweat ran down our backs, lightning bugs pushed through the still air creating little bits of magic we tried to capture in mayonnaise jars. One night Laura found it easier to take them out of my container and transfer them into hers. A chase ensued. There might have been a push, and Laura ended up on the ground with broken glass. That memory was stitched into her arm.

I was also responsible for the scar slicing through my sister Jennifer's right eyebrow. She was attempting to change the channel on our tiny TV encased in a wooden box. I shoved her, and she hit the corner of the console.

I'd rather be remembered for carrying my youngest sister Pam in my arms to Doctor Collaside's office at the end of our street after I heard her screams when her bare foot got caught in the spokes of Suzan's bicycle. They were sitting on the steps of a neighbor's house when I reached them. Suzan was distraught trying to comfort our four- year-old sister.

And there were the times I carried Suzan to the bathroom if my mother wasn't around. She had rheumatic fever and for a year wasn't supposed to walk. Thirteen months apart, we were almost the same size. My father used to contribute to Boys' Town. I was always impressed by the picture of a boy with his brother on his back and the saying, "He's not heavy, he's my brother." Why not a sister?

We lived at the bottom of a hill, which made learning to stop on roller skates and bikes critical. Scabs on elbows and knees were expected. I remember wildly grabbing hedges and shrubs to slow myself down, my skate key swinging around my neck as I barreled down the street. The soles of our shoes were paper thin from dragging a foot on the sidewalk before mastering the brakes on our Schwinns.

A my name is Alice, and my husband's name is Al, we're here from Alabama to sell you Apples. Legs thrown over the bouncing pink Spalding ball as the refrain singsonged down the street. Hula Hoops and Double Dutch were dominated by the girls. Hopscotch was as regular as peanut butter and jelly.

Three neighborhood fathers cleared the vacant lot behind their houses and planted grass for a great communal playing field. Neighing and galloping, we played at being horses up and down the green stretch inhaling the fresh wild garlic smell of newly mowed grass.

Spying was a favorite pastime. Sometimes we'd crawl on our bellies through our neighbor's shaded garden on the ivy carpet to watch the carp glide golden and shimmer silver in the clear pond. There was a forbidden place near the railroad tracks we called *Mystery Winds* where we jumped between islands with water swirling around them. Looking back I think it was a water treatment plant.

We had several clubhouses. One was a lean-to made out of appliance-sized cardboard boxes propped up over a low cement wall in the back of the gas station on the corner of our block and Northern Boulevard. We covered the dirt floor with magazines, which my sister Jennifer swept every day. Even as a child she was a compulsive cleaner. On the same wooded lot was a girls-only tree house Judy O' Connor's father had built. It was the best, until Judy fell out of the tree and broke her arm.

It seemed that our childhood winters were snow covered. A steep hill that branched around either side of a stone park on Westmoreland Street one block over was a popular place to sled. Before the expression, "Help me I've fallen and I can't get up." became synonymous with senior citizens, it was uttered by any child bundled so tightly into snowsuits that they walked like penguins. Once you were zipped up and snapped into your winter layers there was no in and out, no coming and going.

As we got older, we didn't want to go home before the 5 o'clock curfew even knowing that at the end of the day, pulling off rubber boots and ice encrusted socks, our red feet and numb fingers would start to defrost and burn like hell. This was similar to the kind of self-inflicted torture in the summer when you'd stay in the ocean until your fingers pruned and your salty baby tits stung when they rubbed against your bathing suit.

Nassau Road was a mixed neighborhood in the 1950s: Von Burgsdorf, O'Connor, Belaforie, Kosick, Firestein, Egan, McGowan, Schlutz, Borsoff. As a gang we played catch-a-flier up in the middle of our lightly traveled street.

Before we were teenagers and no longer interested in the boys on the block, there was flirting and teasing and testing. The boys sent around a rating sheet of the neighborhood girls assigning us numbers from 1 to 10 for looks and personality. My archrival Pat Egan had a dimple in the middle of her chin and a perfect page boy. She and I did well with 9s and 10s. However, we felt that the boys were less than generous to some of the younger girls. So we decided to return the favor with not just numbers but comments as well. Suzan Kosick offered to type our rebuttal. We had initialed our comments, but for some reason she eliminated all the initials but mine.

After a few days with no response, I called my shadow, Herbie Von Burgsdorf, to find out what was going on. He put his mother on the phone, and she accused me of ruining her oldest son Billy's reputation. She was a fierce woman who wielded a wooden spoon when she screamed, "Billy, Herbie, get in here." if they weren't home on the dot of 5. So I laid low for a while and stayed at my end of the block.

Most neighbors did not have an open door policy, but I was a regular at Judy O'Connor's house. Judy had thick auburn hair cut in Buster Brown fashion; horn-rimmed glasses sat at the top of her freckled nose. Judy was the smartest in her class at the best public school on Long Island. She had a younger sister and brother.

Her reed thin grandmother, Mrs. Hotchkiss, lived with them. She wore elegant floral print dresses and was a rabid baseball fan, which seemed so unladylike. I pictured her when no one was around swinging her silver-tipped cane like a bat.

I admired Mrs. O' Connor who garnished ice tea with mint from her well-tended border alongside the driveway. For Judy's birthday one year she create a Currier and Ives dinner party featuring a golden roast turkey on a platter surrounded by sugar coated grapes and an Angel Food birthday cake dripping chocolate icing. Birthdays were celebrated unceremoniously at our house.

At Christmas although our unwrapped piles of presents were mountainous, Judy's were either beautifully wrapped or in Lord and Taylor boxes.

Judy's father was a lawyer; I rarely saw him and then he just disappeared. I overheard my mother whispering to a neighbor, "She should have looked the other way." I couldn't understand why anyone wouldn't want to live at O' Connor's house.

At the tender age of ten, I ran away. Mrs. O' Connor found me sitting on their attic stairs and convinced me to go home. Three years later Judy sent her mother into the upstairs bathroom when I had discovered blood on my underpants.

To paraphrase Mr. Rogers, It was a wonderful day in the neighborhood when masked men like Zorro, The Lone Ranger and Superman were the good guys. Nassau Road was our nest, a safe place to test your wings because if you fell, someone was there to pick you up.

Back to School

Like a mini New Year's Eve, the first day of a new month generally fills me with enthusiasm and motivation, but the beginning of September means the end of summer. Despite the fact that it isn't officially over for twenty two days, that the weather will continue to be gorgeous, and that water temp will be at its warmest, summer is over. It's like the end of a relationship. It might drag on, but you know in your heart it's done.

I park next to the pavilion at the ocean and stroll towards the bridge. Swallow flight school is in session. It must be an intermediate class because they have graduated from short liftoffs and landings in the parking lot to excursions over the dunes.

On Tuesday I will be waiting at the bus stop with my granddaughter Gabrielle for her first day at pre-K and her brother Jeremy's kindergarten debut. Then I'll drive over to their cousin Jayden's house a few blocks away to hug my grandson before he becomes a student for the first time.

I remember my sunny faced daughter Melissa skipping onto the school bus on her first day of kindergarten. She didn't look back. There's a photo of Ashley, her brother, waiting for the bus. I am standing with my arms folded across my chest, tears hidden behind sunglasses. All that is visible of Ashley is his little hand on my thigh.

While wading through old photos, I found a black and white class snapshot of my class dated February 1955. In the corner is the number 56 students. To squeeze us in for the camera, there are only four rows of eight desks, with holes for ink wells. The remaining 26 students are lined up like Dominoes along the back and window walls.

It amazes that when I look at the faces, names start flipping like a Rolodex through my mind: Rosemarie Meyer, Muriel Doyle, Larry Larkin. Lucy somebody is holding the sign with our information. Saint Anastasia. Douglaston, NY. Sister Mary. Grade 4A. Denise Fenton is the only other person I'll know for years with the same first name. She is beside Marcella Lundy whose name I always admired. There must have been some special dispensation for picture day since we aren't wearing our non-descript uniform jumpers with white shirts, which only look good on the eighth grade girls with pointy cone shaped bras.

My eyes move up and down the aisles. I spot Peter Bruschi and his twin sister Madeline; Valerie Kurtz, Patty McCaffrey, some of the smart girls; and Tommy Hogan, one of the goofy boys.

There's shy Mary Genussa. Since we were placed in alphabetical order I usually sat behind her. After she tired of complaining about me borrowing pencils, we became friends. She explained to me exactly what sexual intercourse meant. Her mother verified.

A future success, Frank Honnercamp, wearing a jacket and bow tie, anchors the last seat in the last row. Handsome Richie Carmella, in a cowboy shirt and a tie is the first along the 12-foot windows. Next in a Howdy Dowdy outfit is Herbie Von Burgsdorf who lived on my block and was glued to my side. Red-headed white-faced Bill Perry is seated in the middle of the class smiling. A big improvement from kindergarten when he threw up every morning.

I imagine that a lot of Catholic school kids developed stomach and digestive problems, especially if a nun like Sister Fides ruled the cafeteria. We would file into the cavernous room in orderly double lines to assigned seats. After we said grace she clicked her metal clicker, the type used to train dogs, and we could be seated. If there was too much noise, she'd double click and the whole process started again.

When lunch ended, monitors stationed at the garbage pails ripped open our brown bags and made sure we had finished our lunch. No food wasted. We were constantly told to think of the starving children in China. I was a slow eater. After getting caught several times, I started packing just half a peanut butter and jelly sandwich on Wonder Bread. I didn't hit 100 pounds until I was in high school.

One day I forgot my lunch. A kind nun took pity on me. She led me to the convent where I sat on cement steps and ate a roast beef sandwich on rye bread with olives on the side and ice tea. It made me consider a vocation.

During the years at Saint Anastasia, we were inoculated with the polio vaccine. The fear of becoming crippled or having to spend your life in an iron lung was enough to keep us out of community swimming pools. Meanwhile there was the threat of THE bomb and a

Cold War being raged around us. I still have the tarnished dog tags we wore for identification purposes in case we were attacked by the Commies. I guess they realized that huddling in a hallway with our arms over our heads or crouching under our desks wasn't a bomb-proof solution.

❖❖❖❖❖

Back in the Ponquogue Beach parking lot, the swallows explode from the bramble and pepper the sky with dark confetti. After a short exploration period, the undulating swarm is vortexed into dense shrub thickets. The drill is repeated again and again.

Northern Boulevard

Even from a distance on the Ponquogue Bridge I can see the bay knuckling into the jetty. The Hurricane of 1938 ripped an inlet through the barrier beach physically separating Hampton Bays from Southampton. The towns are now connected by two bridges over the Shinnecock Canal. You often hear the expression east or west of the canal, which suggests two states of mind as well as a direction.

In my young mind the invisible city line that separated my town from the one next to it divided worlds. From 5 to 16, I lived in suburban Great Neck one block east of city line. But I spent most of my time in Little Neck where a close city type of life brewed. Until high school my world revolved around the mile from my house to St Anastasia on Northern Boulevard in Little Neck where I went to church and school with my cousins.

When I was a preteen, I ventured off Nassau Road that was three blocks long and tested my freedom on Northern Boulevard. Instinctively I ran past the bar on the corner with my head down making no eye contact with the men sitting at the window. Mangel's Deli next to a vacant lot was one of the first stops. I spent my allowance there on potato salad with thin white dressing peppered with very finely chopped parsley and dill pickles quartered and wrapped in white paper.

Errands with my father generally meant going to the "chinks" for his starched shirts and handkerchiefs. The sign on the door said, "No tickie no shirtie." He never had a ticket, but my father always walked out with a bundle wrapped in brown paper and tied with white string. Next was Mr. Sitabart's, the dry cleaner shop with heavy smells and a hint of cigars. The Buster Brown shoe store was in the middle of town. We were steady customers, since my father negotiated a family discount. Counting the five of us, there were twenty-eight children between my father's brothers and sister who lived within a three-mile radius off Northern Boulevard in Little Neck.

Saint Anastasia Church, rectory, con-vent and grammar school with a big cement play-ground and parking lot dominated several city blocks and most of our young lives. My sisters and I each had at least one cousin in our grade who celebrated First Communions, Confirmations and graduations together. There were lots of older cousins, so no one ever messed with us. Unlike our cousins, we took the bus to school because we lived a mile and a fraction away. I always envied the walkers. They were released first and seemed to be more independent.

Sometimes when my cousin Hedy was with us after church, we were allowed to walk part way home. When my father stopped at the bakery, which was one of the few stores open on Sunday, he'd let us get out of the car to stroll home along Northern Boulevard in our Sunday clothes. We'd stand in front of Virginia Variety's window, press our foreheads on the glass, cup hands on either side of our eyes and list things we wanted for the next rainy day: coloring books, paper dolls and bags of the colored cloth we used to weave pot holders on metal frames.

When I was in eighth grade the Brooklyn Diocese split at city line and east of it became Rockville Center Diocese. The big deal for me was that most of the kids in my class and my cousins would not be going to my high school since they lived on the other side of city line in Little Neck.

The kids on my block went to public school. I took a bus ten miles east to St. Mary's in Manhasset, where the boys in a separate building sported crew cuts and wore blazers. A world away from city line. It was then that I began to realize that we were the rich ones, the spoiled Gray girls, fancy car, and summers in the Hamptons. Yet when we moved further east to more affluent town, I felt like my slip was showing.

I preferred hoody boys like my first crush Bobby Carmella. Like caramel his name melted in my mouth. Blond curls greased into a DA, toffee colored skin, he wore tight jeans and a black leather jacket that hung loosely on his taut frame. His younger brother Richie was in my elementary class. The Carmella boys lived with their pretty mother in an apartment over the appliance store on Northern Boulevard in Little Neck; I never remember seeing their father.

Sid's candy store was Bobby's hangout, which was convenient for me since it was next door to Mangel's Delicatessen. If my timing was right, he and his boys would be jumping off the Q12 bus, cigarettes dangling from their lips, as I was walking to the deli.

Occasionally, Bobby came into the store to buy milk or bread for his mother. So I would stall for time by stuffing the Miss Rheingold ballot box, just in case he might appear.

After I graduated from grammar school, I decided that it was time to hang out at Sid's for a coke and eventually a Parliament pilfered from my mother's purse. Perched in my uniform on the faded red plastic covered stools that squeaked as I spun, I was branded a Catholic school girl.

Sid's store was long and narrow. It smelled like a bar without the beer odor; I was comfortable there. The walls on one side were lined with magazines, newspapers, and comic books. I was an *Archie and Veronica* fan. On the other side Sid held court at the laminate counter next to the glass enclosed cases of cigars and cigarettes behind the cash register. The male conversations revolved around the Brooklyn Dodgers, world affairs and local gossip. I basically listened. After a while I'd say hi to Bobby who never offered me more than a disarming smile. His husky friend, Stevie Goldberg, who wore glasses held together with a band aid across the bridge of his nose, occasionally talked at me if no one else was around.

In the beginning of sophomore year, it was time to expand my world. On Friday afternoons I boarded the Q12 bus on Northern Boulevard. I listened to the clicking sound of my change funnel down the fare box and then took a seat by the window as we passed Virginia Variety's, Shaffer's Funeral Parlor, Howard Johnson's, Carvel and Saint Anastasia, heading west towards Flushing ten miles away.

I met a group of friends at Jahn's Ice Cream Parlor where I ordered lime Rickeys and smoked Marlboros. By the end of the school year it became a meeting place for me and my first love. We also spent many Saturday nights necking in the last row of the Little Neck Movie Theater through newsreels, cartoons and double features, especially on freezing winter nights. After he walked me home, he'd hop on the Q12 to Bayside, and then jog three miles to his house.

At the end of my junior year in high school, my family moved farther east from Great Neck to a larger house in Garden City where you couldn't walk to town, or hang out at a candy store, or take a bus to be with friends. You needed a car to get around; kids had less freedom. With one year left, I continued at St. Mary's and then went to college in Philadelphia.

When I am asked, "Where did you grow up?" I usually say, "Great Neck and Garden City." I *should* say Northern Boulevard.

Wakes and Funerals

As I walked along the fence of the Coast Guard Station towards the Ponquogue Bridge, I notice corks from wine bottles rolling about. Last night's strong wind must have whirled like a mini tornado into the urns at the entrance to the Inn Spot across the street depositing the corks willy nilly. Instead of thinking of the lovely wines I have imbibed, my mind goes to the expression, "put a cork in it" and to our family funerals.

With the death of Aunt Mary in 2006, my cousins and I have become the front line. Wakes and funerals are our family reunions. After each death we insert a cork in our grief, but it ferments and sometimes pops at the next gathering. The heaviness of our history is buoyed with humor and alcohol and drugs. At this stage a third are in the program, a third should be and the final third is just lucky.

The first wake I remember was Nana's, my father's mother. I happened to be in the car with him one afternoon when he stopped to visit her. I probably didn't know that she was sick because children were spared those conversations. Nana was floating around the room in a long white cotton nightgown, her dark hair loose down her back. She seemed to have turned into a child. My father picked her up in his arms and put her back in bed. Months later I was ushered into Shaffer's Funeral Parlor off Northern Boulevard to kiss her waxen cheek and then brought home.

Some of my fondest memories were at Nana's house. Nana and Aunt Betsy lived next door to Aunt Mary on the corner of 248th Street and Depew Avenue. Two impressive sets of cement steps partially shaded by sagging spruces sat ignored in the front of the house. Everyone used the side door that entered into the kitchen. There you could often find Aunt Betsy filling coupon books, sitting at the table with a quart bottle of Piels and a box of cellophane wrapped Raleigh cigarettes. Half of their possessions were acquired with Raleigh coupons and S&H Green Stamps.

Since Nana's house was too small and the family too big, we visited in shifts at Christmas drifting in and out to give and receive presents. Nana would say, "You're George's oldest." I don't think she remembered my name.

But at Nana's Friday night cousins' party for the younger grandchildren we all felt special. Crowded around her plastic covered dining room table, we played Bingo for pennies while sipping soda, a rare treat in our house. We also rolled dice and bet on a horse racing game. Cheating was rampant. Nana sat at the head of the table and ran the show.

The best part was when it was your turn to stay overnight with your favorite cousin and sleep in the big bed in the wallpapered bedroom in the front of the house. After all the kids left with melting ice pops, my cousin Hedy and I sat on the slipcovered couch wedged between Aunt Betsy and Nana in house dresses that exposed their flabby arms. We watched *Gunsmoke,* which wasn't over until 11 o'clock.

Hedy's father, Uncle Henry, head usher at Saint Anastasia, was the first uncle to die. Farther up 248th Street my father's sister Evelyn and her red-headed husband, Henry, raised five girls and one boy in a three bedroom house with an enclosed porch and a basement. It was never quite clear where everyone slept. The older girls, Kathleen and Evelyn, looked like the pinups on 1950s calendars standing on tip toes in two piece bathing suits. Both had gorgeous lifeguard boyfriends whom they would marry and live happily ever after. Beth was a few years older than I, which back then was a generation. Hedy was in the class ahead of me. Her sister Jackie was the baby. Their brother, Georgie, and I were born in the same year, 1946.

Although I sat with my cousins at Uncle Henry's wake trying to understand what you were supposed to do or feel, my parents wouldn't let me go to my uncle's funeral because they thought I was too young. I was furious. Georgie and I were both in eighth grade. There are photos of the two of us side by side at our first Holy Communion, Confirmation and graduation from Saint Anastasia Elementary School. He was my special cousin. After high school George went to Vietnam and was never the same after he came home.

Like his father, he died in his fifties. There was a subdued memorial for him. Richie Carmella and a few other classmates from St. Anastasia attended.

None of the many family wakes have been as dramatic as Billy's, Aunt Mary's youngest. He was so young. Not dying in the proper order. The child before the parent. Twenty-five-year-old Billy was waked with a stuffed armadillo in his casket. It made more sense than rosary beads wound around steepled hands. The reckless rugby player lost control of his jeep and smashed into a tree after a Billy Joel concert in Montauk.

At Billy's funeral, his sister Ann stood at the pulpit and after a few words in her throaty voice; she raised her arm, pumped it and yelled, "Let's give it to Billy like he gave it to us." The church exploded with hoots and cheers and a thunderous stamping of feet that echoed through the cathedral like Saint Aloysius as the parish priest stood in surprised dismay.

The last I saw Aunt Mary alive was at her daughter Ann's baby shower at the New York City Athletic Club. Despite the fact that the party was a no smoking area, my Aunt lit one cigarette after another and had glasses of wine queued in front of her. I figured at this point in her life she could do whatever she pleased.

Her husband Frank, my father's youngest brother, died before he turned fifty leaving my Aunt Mary a widow and pregnant with her tenth child. Billy. It seemed such a common name after her ninth baby, India.

At the shower in a banquet room softened by balloons and the piles of pastel wrapped presents, there was a line for the fortune teller behind a screen in a corner of the room. I wonder if she would have predicted that Aunt Mary would lose three children to early deaths. Her daughters Joan and Barbara would follow Billy. One stalked by cancer, the other by drugs.

There are no more aunts and uncles alive. It is us who are dying now. We are burying our cousins, our peers.

Wakes and funerals bring us together to catch up and to reminisce about the days on 248th Street. We share an easy sweetness and love that says we are forever family. We are there for one another to laugh, to cry, and for some of us to raise a glass.

High School BFF

My short walk is over. I have to get home to meet the plumber. Several seagull feathers are scattered here and there. In the old days, before I worried about things like mites, I would have put them in my hair.

A truck rumbles by on the Ponquogue Bridge. Looking up, I notice a DiCarlo Food Service van, which makes me think of my friend Madeline whose late husband's name was DiCarlo. Just recently, I received a notice about a high school reunion next year dubbed Senior Spring Break in Orlando. I know that Madeline Mondo DiCarlo, my best friend from Saint Mary's, has probably been planning it for months. She supplied the tiaras, sunglasses and tee shirts for our 50th in Fort Lauderdale. The main reason I go to the reunions is to see her.

The gathering that reunited us was the 35th reunion. Except for Madeline, I didn't expect our crew to be there. Our closest friends during those years were the ones we met in our freshman homeroom: Kathy, Mary Ellen, Mary Francis, Mary, Rosemarie. They were as unique as the five fingers on my hand.

We all came from different towns. We lacked the roots that connect kids who grow up together in the same community: knowing each other's' families, belonging to the same church, attending the same functions. After graduation, like ripened milk weed pods that have burst open exposing the silky fiber wings, they went wherever the wind took them. Madeline and I remained.

On an April afternoon painted with early spring fuzz, buds on the fruit trees still holding their jackets tight, I followed the winding drive to a North Shore Country Club for the 35th reunion of the Class of 1963. Walking into the main reception room, I looked around and thought, "Who are these older women?" With the help of name tags, voices and smiles, years melted away, and we were seventeen again.

As I walked out onto the veranda shaded by a green and white striped awning, I heard Madeline's easy laugh before I saw her. Around the corner there she was in a black sleeveless dress exposing her fleshy arms and plump cleavage, with a boa wrapped around her neck. A very short haircut and a dark tan accentuated her large pale blue eyes that widened when she saw me. In a flash we were a duo again. Nothing in life has changed the fact that we will always be high school best friends.

Before we were seated in alphabetical order on our first day at Saint Mary's Girls' High School in 1963, Madeline had leaned across the aisle and asked if I wanted to have lunch with her. Early on, we decided to sit at a different table every day; we crossed lines of class and cliques. After freshman year we were in different classes, but we were both elected to student council and proudly wore the arm band on our navy blue blazers.

Sports Night was an annual competition extravaganza. St. Mary's was a parish school in affluent Manhasset that accepted tuition paying students according to entrance exam scores. In the acceptance letters each student was assigned to either the blue team or the white team. Two seniors were chosen to be the captains of each team as well as a dozen leaders. This elite group was dominated by the Manhasset girls, many of whom had been together since kindergarten. Madeline and I were happily surprised when we were selected as leaders for the blue team.

There was an incident with Madeline that I wasn't so proud of. We went on a double date to the movies with boys we met at a freshman dance. Halfway through the first feature, Madeline and I excused ourselves to go to the Ladies Room. Looking into the mirror as we teased our hair Madeline asked, "Do you like the guy you're with?"

I shrugged, "He's okay, kind of boring."

Madeline got closer to me and whispered, "Mine's a dud. Let's leave." And we did. I vaguely recall meeting a guy Madeline knew who drove us home.

At our last reunion, I asked Madeline if she remembered that ill-fated date. She did. I cried, "That was so mean. I can't believe we did it. Those guys were probably scarred for life."

Madeline lowered her voice, crooked her index finger and imparted her usual wisdom. "Let me tell you something. More likely it toughened them up. I've had my ego crushed. Not everyone is going to like us."

Madeline lived in Mineola, a town near Garden City, and often picked me up for school our senior year. I was a year younger and didn't have my license yet. She always managed to have a car and cash. Before she had her own car she borrowed a relative's or a boyfriend's or a neighbor's, which she drove with her left leg crossed over her right. Comfortable with adults, she ran errands to local stores for our principal during school hours.

On a sticky June morning that felt like summer vacation was way overdue, Madeline picked me up for school. "Look in the backseat. I have something for you." There in a cardboard box were two glasses and the makings of highballs. We both did well on our science final.

The summer after our senior year Madeline and I got jobs at Fortunoffs, in the bowels of the basement. There was no slot in my brain to register the cast of characters we found there.. A heavy-set woman with a megaphone voice kept us up to date about the boil she had in a delicate area. Our young male manager gave detailed accounts of his girlfriend cooking for him in nothing but an apron. I mentioned to Madeline that one of the guys smelled like chicken soup. She said, "Denise, that's B.O." I learned a lot that summer.

We chose the unglamorous job of working the machines that pinned the price tags on merchandise because we didn't have to work on the weekends. At home she helped her maiden Aunt Ami scrub the house and cook for the week. Then she was free to go to Jones Beach with me during the day and stay out late with our boyfriends at night.

At our reunion one of our classmates told me that she always thought that Madeline and I were such an unlikely pair. I responded, "Like oil and vinegar." I think how different my reserved Irish household was compared to Madeline's Italian family where no topic of conversation was considered taboo or impolite.

Madeline and her younger sister, who lost their mother when they were young, shared a modest house with their father, an unmarried aunt and two bachelor uncles. I lived with my parents and four younger sisters in a gracious house where we each had our own bedroom. At the breakfast table we lined up cereal boxes in front of our bowls, so we didn't have to watch each other eat. My parents generally didn't have dinner with us except on Sundays.

My favorite times with Madeline were spent at her home. Uncle Frank, who was crippled with polio, whiled away his days in a wheelchair at the window when he wasn't crashing around on his crutches. He told jokes constantly. Madeline's older twin cousins, hair set with bobby pins and covered with babushkas, lived next door. They wore cardigans buttoned backward with tight toreador pants and were a source of great information. I knew the facts of life; Madeline filled in the details. Mondo was an appropriate surname for Madeline; she was the worldliest person I had ever met.

Eating at the Mondo's was a treat since my mother's menus were limited and often included Campbell's Soup concoctions. Squeezed in at the Formica-topped kitchen table with her father, Joe, sister Christine, Aunt Ami, Uncle Frank and Uncle Ralph, I learned to remove the outer leaves of a stuffed artichoke, scrape them against my front teeth and suck the edges before I feasted on the sausage and cheese stuffing. I learned to savor food. To take my time. To use mussel shells like spoons. To soak up any remaining liquid with bread. To prepare string beans aioli. To drink water or wine, not milk, with my meal. To listen. To laugh. On holidays, dinners began at 2:00. I would join the family hours later for pastries, nuts, fruit, after dinner drinks and coffee around a long table set up in their basement.

College was the beginning of a change in our friendship. Madeline stayed home and planned to go to nursing school; I went to Chestnut Hill College in Philadelphia. In the 1960s long distance phone calls were for emergencies and special occasions. Madeline did come to visit my freshman year; everyone loved her. After sophomore year, we took a road trip to the Jersey shore where my college friends rented cheap apartments, waitressed and partied for the summer. Madeline brought a cooler filled with gravy and meatballs. I packed my tooth brush and a two piece madras bathing suit.

By the end of my junior year I was engaged to a man Madeline had never met. The first place I went to share the news was her house. She was in my wedding party, but not part of my life after I got married. We lived at opposite ends of Long Island with life happening in between. Birthday notes and Christmas cards kept us loosely connected. Neither one was willing to cut the cord.

Madeline got her nursing degree, married and divorced her high school sweetheart. She moved to Bridgeport, Connecticut, with her second husband where she has spent most of her adult life. Later in her career Madeline became a forensic nurse, the one you would want if you were ever the victim of a violent crime. She never had children. I missed the last reunion because it coincided with the birth of our sixth grandchild.

❖❖❖❖❖

It's time, I think, as I look out at the expanse of water and back again to the beach where the oldest tier of seaweed is bleached white like shredded paper. The newest layer still black and wet. It's time for one of us to get on that ferry and cross Long Island Sound.

Bookends

When I leave the house this morning to walk the bridge, I enter a November landscape of falling leaves, skeletal branches and muted colors. Gaudy October is gone and winter is around the corner. Attracted by the scent of burning wood, I stop and watch the smoke from my neighbor's chimney dueling with the cold air. It makes me think of my old friend.

Remember the Brownie ditty, "Make new friends but keep the old. One is silver and the other is gold."? There is a certain comfort that comes with friends who knew you when you were just you, before all the trappings and titles. The ones who remind you of mistakes you made in your first marriage, so you don't repeat them. Other than my sisters, Pam Mack has been my constant lifelong friend.

We just spent two nights with Pam and her husband, Steve at their home in Columbia, Maryland. Pam doesn't smell or look like a smoker with the wrinkled pursed skin around the mouth and pruning of the face, but I can hear it in her breathing and in her raspy voice. Since she doesn't invite her habit indoors, her house doesn't smell like an ashtray, but her car does. She still smokes. And I got her started.

Pam and I attended the same high school, but we really weren't friends until the beginning of senior year when my family moved to Garden City. Waiting for the school bus, we stood in our Saint Mary's uniforms under a maple tree in September 1962 before fall's alchemy had begun. There were a handful of us. I was eating a graham cracker, since breakfast was not a mandatory meal in our house. I turned to Pam who was standing next to me hugging her books to her chest, "Hey Pam, I have a permit, and you have a license. My father's Volkswagen Bug is parked at the train station. I think we should become friends. What do you say?"

I can still picture us in my yellow Bug or her blue Skylark convertible driving down the tree named streets in Garden City in the spring of our lives with cigarettes cradled between index and middle fingers.

In ninth grade I began stealing Parliaments or Kents from my mother's pocketbook to practice my technique in front of the bathroom mirror while fanning the smoke out the open window. The sensuous look I was aiming for eluded my thin-lipped mouth. My high school boyfriend, who blew perfect smoke rings, was a Marlboro man. I graduated to a real smoker when I stopped grubbing his and bought my own.

At college I was a regular in the only room where we were permitted to indulge our habit. It seems hard to imagine in today's world, but in 1968 I inhaled a pack of cigarettes in the labor room before my daughter was born. The previous year as a bride I had promised my mother that I wouldn't smoke in my wedding gown.

Pam knows that I hate the fact that she hasn't quit, but we don't talk about it anymore. I used to feel guilty that I initiated her into the cool world of smoking, encouraging her first drags, supplying her habit and insisting that she inhale, but that was a long time ago. It took me nine months after my daughter was born to give up the addiction.

During our recent visit, I began to wonder how much time she spends daily in pursuit of a nicotine fix. She has this handy dandy portable ashtray, a permanent fixture on her front porch. At least when cigarette smoking was fashionable, we smoked in the comfort of our homes and crystal ashtrays heavy enough to kill someone graced our coffee tables. I snuck a shot on my phone camera of her sitting outside bundled in her fleece cocoon robe grabbing the first cig of the day.

One of my favorite photos is from Christmas 1969. Pam and I are standing in front of my parents' fireplace with our seven-month pregnant bellies touching. After she and Steve moved out of state, we saw each other whenever she came home to visit her parents.

On my husband's bedside table is a framed picture taken of Terry and I dancing at Pam and Steve's daughter's wedding in 2008. During the reception at the Baltimore Museum of Practical Things, there was a special cake presentation for Pam and Steve who were celebrating their 40th anniversary. They announced that their Matron of Honor was at the wedding and called me up to stand with them as they cut the cake.

For over 50 years Pam and I have been witnesses to each other's lives. I sent her three dozen roses for her thirty-sixth wedding anniversary to make up for the ones I had forgotten. She called me to share that she going to be inducted into the Howard County Women's Hall of Fame and asked for advice about what to wear. Pam's wardrobe consists of turtle necks, fleece jackets, or quilted vests in every color with matching accessories. "Wear the purple dress, not the black, important jewelry, and forget the sensible shoes." I sat with her family on the night of the ceremony.

Pam's mother, a diminutive chain smoker, died in her early 60s of ovarian cancer. Pam stood at the podium on the altar at Saint Joseph's Church in Garden City and began the eulogy. "My mother was Auntie Mame with strong religious convictions." It was one of the bravest things I could imagine. It gave me the courage, which I don't think I would have had, to do the same for my mother.

When my mother died four years after my father, I was 50, divorced and alone. Pam came and stayed with me for five days while I blubbered through old stories and boxes of Kleenex. She drove to restaurants, so I could drink as many cocktails as I liked, and brought me water and Aspirin in the morning. Always the businesswoman, she estimated the bottom line of what my sisters and I would inherit and what being an executrix would involve.

She also confessed that she didn't expect a long life since her mother died young and Pam had had a few medical problems. If that happened, she wanted me to marry Steve. She knew I would be good to her children and would rather have me than some unknown enjoy her life savings. I don't think Steve had been consulted.

On the last night of our visit, we sat like bookends at either end of her family room couch, our legs parallel, and our wine glasses refilled, we talked about the fact that time is playing on the other side now. Pam said how relieved she was when she passed her 63rd birthday, the age when her mother, Peg, died. A year older than I, my dear friend will turn 70 next year. She claimed that she isn't afraid of dying. Her life has been good, and she would die happy.

I don't think she intends to give up smoking, but I have witnessed enough ironies in life to not be surprised if Pam outlives her athletic, yoga practicing husband. I told her I'm not afraid of death,

I'm afraid of being sick. "Yeah, I know what you mean." She agreed and began to cough.

In Sync

I am not walking the bridge alone today. In my pocket is the new iPhone 6. My first smart phone is keeping track of how many miles I walk, how many steps I take. It does a lot more, but it will take me a while to figure out what and how. I am trying to catch up with modern technology. However I feel out of sync, like how I felt until I reached the age of reason, somewhere in my forties.

My feeling out of sync began in kindergarten. Back then my school had two terms with students graduating from eighth grade in January as well as in June. I was four-years-old when I entered Kindergarten in the beginning of 1951. In seventh grade, in order to eliminate January graduations, we were accelerated a half a year. My fate was sealed. I would not be in the grade I should have been. I would always be a year younger than my classmates.

The day I turned thirteen at the end of 8th grade I was playing horses, galloping up and down the field behind our neighbors' houses tossing my hair and neighing. Suddenly it dawned on me. I was a teenager. I threw down the invisible reins and walked home

I thought I had the age thing mastered in my head, but my body didn't cooperate. St. Mary's High School uniform helped to disguise the fact that I was under a hundred pounds and hadn't menstruated yet. Eventually the hormones kicked in along with a boyfriend.

When I was a senior, my parents laid out a map of the east coast on our kitchen table and drew a small circle telling me that I could consider colleges within that circumference. In 1963 if you attended a Catholic high school and your parents could afford the tuition, the next stop was Catholic college. Except for a few nursing programs, co-ed Catholic universities didn't exist. I chose Chestnut Hill College in Philadelphia because it was surrounded by men's schools. I didn't want to be stuck in the woods in a convent, and besides part of the purpose of higher education was to earn an MRS.

During my four years at Chestnut Hill, there were few changes other than curfew hours. We were encapsulated in a white-gloved, silver-tea-service world while the beginnings of social and political upheaval rumbled beyond the campus.

Freshman year President John F. Kennedy was assassinated. Running late for Mr. Rey's French class, I realized that everyone was moving in the opposite direction. Some of the girls were crying. A friend grabbed me and told me the news. Within minutes the entire school filled the chapel.

The scariest part was I couldn't get in touch with my parents that day. Twenty girls shared one pay phone. When it was finally my turn, the circuits were down. As freshmen we weren't allowed to go home until Thanksgiving vacation. Classes were canceled. We sat around the small black and white TV in the smoker and watched endless news coverage.

After twenty-four depressed hours, the phone rang and like a takeout order a male voice boomed, "We need ten girls for a Villanova house party." Mourning was over; college social life began.

One day during my sophomore year Sister Mary Kieran, who lived on Hogan's Alley, our corridor, found me in bed surrounded by college brochures. She asked what I was doing. I told her that CHC wasn't the right place for me. I wanted men and diversity. She laughed, "You'd end up with same kind of friends you have now. It seems to me you have enough dates and with your grades you aren't going anywhere." Except for this bit of rebellious thinking, I loved my time within the granite walls, surrounded by idyllic grounds and near a cobblestoned town.

At the end of my junior year, I was one of the first "lucky girls" to become engaged when weddings were the next party after graduation in June of 1967. Most of us were already having sex with our fiancés. The fact that it was unprotected made it less of a sin. If I got pregnant, it didn't matter very much because I was in love and planned to get married anyway.

We women ran the show at school. I think we assumed we could run the world, but in 1967 the world wasn't ready for us. I used to daydream about becoming president of my father's company. If *Mad Men*, an AMC show about the advertising world in the 60s, is any indication of what it was like for women in business, I now understand why my father never welcomed his daughters into his office.

It wasn't until after graduation that I grasped that my class, the class of 1967 was on the cusp of huge social and political changes. It was more than the tide changing, it was a tidal wave. My freshman year the Beatles' hit was "I Want to Hold Your Hand." Four years later it was "Strawberry Fields Forever." It was then that I questioned how different my life would have been if I had been in the class of 1968.

David Niven and Deborah Kerr starred in *Prudence and the Pill* in 1968. The pill, once considered obscene and vulgar and certainly not condoned by the church, was becoming a pop culture icon. The girls who were in the class I should have been in embraced the pill postponed marriage and applied to grad school.

Protests of the Vietnam War had escalated. The summer of love and bra burning began while I was on my honeymoon. Weed was wafting in the air. By Woodstock I had a baby and was pregnant with the second and married to a man who threatened divorce if I smoked marijuana.

I gave my mother a copy of Betty Friedan's *The Feminine Mystic*. She said that it was too late for her

He warned, "This stuff is going to backfire on you girls."

I think of my college often when I walk the Ponquogue Bridge because the red roofs of the Hampton Bays Coast Guard Station remind me of the terra cotta clay tiled roofs of my alma mater. For our 45th reunion group emails have started to circulate. I piped up when there was a question about who were the youngsters in our class. I was 17 until the end of freshman year.

How would my life have been different if I was in the class of '68? The one I should have been in. Would I have been a pot head, believed in free love and backpacked across Europe? Or would I have attended grad school, lived in a loft in the city and become my father's partner? Or would I have moved to Vermont, married an environmentally conscious farmer and run the local bookstore? I know I wouldn't have married Jack, but then I wouldn't have my daughter and son. I wouldn't be who I am. Like stepping on a butterfly, history would have been altered.

The year I turned 39 I bought a stack of birthday cards for my school friends that read "Happy Birthday. You're 40 and I'm not." At 66 those extra months are meaningless. In our class of one hundred girls, eleven are dead including on dear friend, Sue Kaufman Codd. My college roommate hasn't been heard from in forty years, and one of my closest friends is struggling with cancer. Since our minds and middles have expanded and we have suffered through the changes, I feel a sense of sisterhood and gratitude with the women who shared those four years frozen in time. I think I will enjoy this upcoming reunion.

❖❖❖❖❖

At our 45th reunion registration I spoke to a women whose name tag read class of 1977, ten years after mine. I asked what her expectations were when she graduated. She replied that initially she wanted to go to grad school, but CHC gave her the confidence to pursue a career in law.

In her address Sister Carol Vale, college president, mentioned our motto Fides, Caritas, Scientia: Faith, Charity and Knowledge. Sister Carol explained the motto further saying, Faith first in ourselves, then to God, our family and community. My friends and I were awe struck. First of all, when I was in school the definition of faith was limited to mean faith in the Catholic Church. The thought of putting ourselves first was heresy. Sister Carol didn't say faith in the Catholic Church, she said in God.

At the luncheon two women were honored for their service and generosity to the college. One was a stunning older woman and the other an attractive openly gay woman dressed in a jacket and tie. The alum, which has included men since the class of 2007, stood and cheered. My classmates and I raised our glasses proud of our alma mater, in sync with the times.

❖❖❖❖❖

A flock of black skimmers blanket Shinnecock Bay. One bird rises up and flies low to the other side of the bridge and one after one they domino until the entire flock has landed on the other side.

Sand Between Your Toes

Two liter Coke bottles, a single flip flop, a pack of Marlboros, and a pizza box litter the Ponquogue Bridge. The summer people are here, and we blame them for the garbage on the roads, the bulging traffic and overflowing restaurants. We call them Citiots or RVs for rude visitors. The pine trees at the end of the bridge even seem to be raising a third finger at the onslaught of the seasonal crowd. But the truth is many of us full-time residents started as summer people.

We got sand between our toes renting for a week, a month, a season. Many of us became homeowners when the price was right and sharing space with beer-bonged friends lost its appeal. Living in the Hamptons is seductive. Some people commute for hours to be able to end their days watching the sunset on the bay, surfing a few waves, or just smelling salt air. Retirement often finds empty nesters selling the big house up the Island because they know their kids are more likely to visit at the beach.

After I was married I wanted to live in the city or at the beach. When my husband and I both got teaching jobs in Port Jefferson, a 45-minute commute didn't deter us from moving to Hampton Bays. I had such fond memories of my summers there.

When I was young the ride from Great Neck to the East End was a pilgrimage. Sunrise Highway went as far east as Patchogue, and the Long Island Expressway ended at Smithtown. The family car was packed with our belongings for the entire summer. We were there to stay, especially since my mother didn't drive. My father spent a few weeks on vacation with us and then traveled out on the weekends. The following year, on her third attempt, my mother passed the road test in Riverhead, got her license, and purchased a beach car.

For the five years before high school, we rented "Tree Top," one of Huggins' cottages that fringed Tiana Bay. I found a photo of my sisters and me crowding around "Uncle Bill" Huggins who lived in the big house behind his summer rentals. He wore wire-rimmed glasses under a wide-brimmed straw hat. In this picture he has on a sleeveless undershirt and belted paint- spattered jeans.

Appalachian like, no haircuts until September, my sunburned sisters are all wearing bathing suits except Jennifer who has shoes and socks that match her outfit. Skinny as seaweed, I am barefoot with well calloused feet. I have one leg bent and resting on the inside of the other like the tree pose in yoga. My mouth is closed, for even then I hated my teeth. Suzan, who doesn't have any front teeth, is smiling broadly with freckled laughter. Laura's head is tilted and she is squinting into the camera with her chipmunk smile and untied shoelaces. Half hidden on Suzan's lap, baby Pam is not yet one. She is so fair that the following year she will have sun blisters like sacks on her back.

There was a tiny bathroom by the front door of our white cottage with blue shutters. I don't remember a tub. There might have been a shower, but we used the outside one, running naked from it to the clothesline for sun-warmed towels. The kitchen had a table and chairs on one side and the appliances on the other, including a refrigerator that wasn't grounded. Pam stored jellyfish in the freezer, and more than once she opened the door in a dripping wet bathing suit and shook with shock.

The best part was the dollhouse-like upstairs with eaved roofs, so low my father couldn't stand up straight. Suzan and I shared the bed under the windows that swung open to either side and looked down onto a porch with built in benches. The bay beckoned beyond.

We could tumble out of "Tree Top" into shallow Tiana Bay. On our faded canvas rafts we'd float over beds of seaweed, the home of short-tempered blue claws, where menacing tank-like horseshoe crabs scraped the bay's bottom. My sisters and I slid off the floats waist high and sunk our feet into the sand bar. We rarely went beyond the safety of that space. There was no lifeguard; we had each other.

Across a stretch of land dotted with wild blueberries was a cove. Some days Suzan and I would escape from our younger sisters and crouch in the tall grasses to spy on the local boys skinny-dipping. When our father took us snapper fishing there, we looked shyly at the boys with bamboo rods and colored bobbers knowing they were tan from head to toe.

Two mulberry trees at either end of a hedge separated the Huggin's house from a sunbaked open field that led to the bulkhead. This was our favorite spot to eat watermelon and spit out the black seeds. I pictured that space someday turning into a patch fat with the summery pink fruit webbed together with green vines. When I wanted to be alone, I'd crawl under the weeping branches of the mulberry tree that draped to the ground like ribbons from a maypole loaded with dark purple berries. It was a great place to hide, shaded and cool.

We shared our summers in Hampton Bays with the McCraves and the Kellys. Joan McCrave was my mother's oldest and best friend. Joan's handsome husband Jimmy, with a wide-toothed smile and bushy eyebrows, was a New York City cop, who because of shift work, was around during the week. He was the one who blew up the tubes, planted the beach umbrellas and confiscated fireworks for us for the 4th of July.

The Kelly's small ranch on Bay Avenue was built with money Mari, my mother's cousin, won on *Two for the Money*, a game show in the 50s. I can picture Mari standing in her kitchen at the counter next to the stove slapping sandwiches together assembly line fashion while she talked nonstop in machine-gun rapid speech.

Mari Louise Kelly, who served as a nurse in World War II, took us on adventures. She'd load her six children and a couple of us dressed in our pajamas into her station wagon with beach chairs strapped to the roof and drive to the Drive-in Movie on Flanders Road, in Riverhead. I had my first fresh water swimming experience, which made me appreciate the buoyancy of salt water, when she introduced us to Trout Pond in Southampton. Since she read all the local papers she knew where the church suppers were, when bingo nights were held and which square dances were children friendly.

Our parents made us take Red Cross swimming lessons at Meschutt Beach, which we nicknamed Jim's Beach after Jimmy McCrave. As soon as the instructions were over, the adults rounded up the kids and herded us to the ocean. My sisters and I all wore red bathing caps and were instructed to stay in front of the lifeguard, Coach Lopez, the high school gym teacher. Since we spent most of our time at the ocean instead of the bay, we rarely swam. You just had to know when to dive under the waves, when to jump over and when to ride them.

In the 1950s you could count the dozen or so families on Ponquogue Beach, not so any more. But the Ponquogue pavilion is still the only building for a mile in either direction, which makes our beach one of the most beautiful in the Hamptons.

When we were kids there was a building with a bathroom, salt water shower and stalls for changing. The one at the end had a peek hole into the boys' side. After a few incidents it was boarded up.

A snack shack sat on the sand next to the changing area. Shutters held up by hooks created an opening where Mrs. Lopez and her older daughter, both blondes, leaned over the counter to wait on customers. My sisters and I scoured the beach collecting bottles to redeem for coins. With two cents for small ones and five for the larger bottle, we purchased penny pretzels, a bottle of Coke or ice cream.

Things have changed over the years. The snack shack had been replaced with the pavilion, where you can't redeem soda bottles for treats. There are three lifeguards instead of one, and the crowd has mushroomed. But when I sink my feet into the sand, walk onto that stretch of beach, drop my chair at the water's edge, I feel at home.

❖❖❖❖❖

Appreciating my history with Hampton Bays, I open the trunk of my car parked at the foot of the bridge and grab a garbage bag and a long handled pick. I decide to tidy up for our visitors who someday, moved by memories of sand between their toes, may join us as year-round residents.

Pruning

On the bridge the sunlight catches a ball of fishing filament turning it into spun silver. A 7-11 coffee cup, a headless killie, and new stains on the cement suggest interlopers who have ignored the "No Fishing" sign on the Ponquogue Bridge.

I understand small infractions of the law. When I was a kid, my mother translated "No Trespassing" signs into "Welcome Betty." Her father owned a real estate agency and although my mother never worked in the business, a curiosity and love of houses and property ran deep in her blood.

After we moved to Garden City she had the habit of driving at a crawl down the streets east and west of Stewart Avenue. She'd point out good architectural bones: leaded glass windows, slate roofs, substantial front doors and the refinement boxwood and pachysandra bring to a garden.

But her favorite forays were off the beaten path in the Hamptons. My sisters and I would flatten our bodies on the back seat of her Buick crying, "No. Mommy, no," as we'd pass the Private Road signs and creep down rutted roads or long driveways while she noted wild flowers and cultivated plants gone awry.

My father too took a casual approach to most rules. Coming home from Westhampton Beach Country Club after dark, he purposefully drove in the middle of the road claiming it was the safest way. This might have accounted for the numerous speeding tickets he accumulated while cruising through the tiny village of Quogue with its ever present police force. And every Mother's Day he'd present my mother with an armful of freshly cut lilacs long before we had a hedge of it running the length of our property. He never revealed his source.

As their firstborn, I like to think I've inherited the best of their renegade genes. When we spent our summers in Hampton Bays, I foraged in my neighbor's garden. Old Man Foster's vegetable patch sat invitingly close to the edge of the beach. On hot sandy days, if his car wasn't in the driveway, like Peter Rabbit I'd help myself to a juicy tomato and pick a cucumber from under a cool leafy bower.

Forty years ago when I was newly married, we built our house on a former cow pasture. Other than grasses and a large oak tree, our property was a blank slate. Professional landscaping wasn't in our budget, so creativity was called for. I suggested that my husband dig up cedar saplings in the vacant acres behind our house and plant them along one side of our property line. Emboldened by his success, I began to scout our neighborhood for future possibilities.

There were six houses on our block that dead ends at Shinnecock Bay; we were the only year-round residents for years. The street remained dark at night until Memorial Day weekend when lights in our neighbors' homes started to spark along with barbeques and Memorial Day fireworks. Summer residents weren't here in the spring. So I didn't think they would miss a few tulips standing tall waiting to be chosen or daffodils that multiplied like rabbits.

At first I just picked furtively watching for witnesses. Early morning seemed safest for my covert operations. Before long, I developed a sense of ownership as a secret caretaker. I realized how much cleaner it was to use clippers for cutting witch hazel followed by forsythia branches to force indoors for a burst of burnt orange and sunshine yellow when winter becomes so long. Who can resist just *touching* pussy willows?

Pruning can become compulsive: just a little more. I didn't want to trim to the extent that my neighbors might notice, so I started carrying a pair of clippers and loppers in my car and broadening my search. The service roads of Sunrise Highway are loaded with crab apple, cherry and dogwood trees.

Closer to home one morning I noticed a clump of blue bearded iris behind a fieldstone stanchion on a former motel property. I figured I would come back with a trowel and give it a happy home with other iris. But someone beat me to it. There wasn't a rhizome or a sword-shaped leaf left. Not to be outdone by competition, I added a small shovel to my arsenal, so when I saw beds of lily of the valley in Southampton in the path of bulldozers waiting to rip up the ground for a foundation, I was prepared to rescue them.

It was handy to have a spade ready to relocate neglected peonies in the back of an abandoned house. I would give them a loving home. Day lilies that ran wild needed a more protective environment for their flamboyant but short-lived lives. Candytuft was unappreciated in a summer house yard, especially those of negligent owners. I did have boundaries. I respected well-kept homes and public places like banks or the library.

If you knew where and when to look on the side of country roads, thickets of raspberries, like ruby thimbles, and brambles of sweet blackberries were there for the picking. My license plate should have read, "I brake for berries."

As the East End's year round and weekend population exploded, my residential pruning fell dormant. I resorted to tramping along railroads tracks for bouquets of sweet pea tendrils, Queen Ann's Lace parasols, and cornflower blue chicory flowers.

Later in life I became content in my own garden, but my farewell additions from someone else's are my crowning glories. Before the screen door slams behind me this morning, I am happy to see the blooming fuchsia day lilies with yellow centers that I dug up from my mother's garden after my father died. Sunny and colorful like my dad, they were his favorites.

That year I helped my mother install a shade garden nestled below the deck off her kitchen with varieties of hosta, astibles, and lily of the valley. All purchased at a nursery.

Four years later after my mother died, I knew I wanted something from her garden. I carried home a large leafed Blue Angel Hosta we had planted together. Trying to find the perfect spot I transplanted it several times. Its final resting place is under the Kousa dogwood in my backyard alongside a brick path.

I have divided it several times to share with others, something both my parents would have appreciated.

Daddy

Sunday morning on the Ponquogue Bridge--my kind of church. Eucharistic sunbeams fill a Blessed Mother blue sky. It's early so silence plays in the background, except I hear giggles. Then I see a little girl, crowned with strawberry curls riding on her father's shoulders. She is perfumed with coconut smelling sun tan lotion sitting on top of the world. My smile turns into tears after they flip flop by.

I miss my father. George Patrick Gray, who was born in June 1918 and died in 1996, was fond of saying that virile men have daughters. He had five. When I tell people that I am one of five girls they automatically say, "Your poor father." I correct them. My mother had the hard job. My father was the king; we idolized him. If you asked who was his favorite, my sisters and I would each say, "I was."

Only one of us is still married to the first husband. That makes me wonder if having a wonderful father sets you up for disappointment when the men in your life can't seem to fill his shoes. I realize that there are many factors that go into a successful marriage and I can't speak for my sisters, but I believe it was true for me.

Dad lived the American Dream. My father left school as an early teen. The nuns berated the tall gangly kid in the back of the room who couldn't read. He couldn't see the blackboard, and there was no money for glasses. The eighth in a family of nine children, his father died when he was four. There was talk about him and his brothers "borrowing" things like bikes when they needed them. He had friends named Bugged Eyed Reynolds and Snot Nose McGee. When he was older, he worked on the docks in New York City harbor and later in Colorado as part of the Civilian Conservation Corps to build the Hoover Dam.

He started as a laborer, but he was destined to become a successful businessman. He once told me that people choose security or money. His older cousin Frank Devlin recognized that George was a natural salesman and told him about a business that was hiring.

My father, a storyteller, loved to share his version of how he started in the company that he eventually owned. According to him, there was a long line of men waiting outside the building where the interviews for a salesman at Lane Office Furniture were taking place. First he bought a high school ring at a pawn shop and then called Charlie Lane, the president of the company, from a phone booth and said, "The man you want to hire is the one at the end of the line."

He was a great provider. My mother was a skilled shopper and dragged us to bargain department stores. But if you went shopping with my father, a rare treat, he drove right to Best & Co. or Lord and Taylor. Once when I couldn't decide which winter coat I liked, he said, "Take both. Let's go." His famous jewelry grab bag filled with five gifts from Fortunoffs and then Tiffany's for his girls at Christmas made us the envy of all our friends. We wanted for nothing.

He was the Santa Claus of the family. Cash appeared when needed. Bail made. Situations were handled. His younger brother borrowed suits and shoes for special occasions. Aunt Evelyn worked for him after Henry died. She married my father's vice president, a widower. Aunt Mary became my father's secretary and ran his office until he retired. He wasn't just generous to us; he tipped people who didn't expect to be, like the man who pumped gas.

He was different from his siblings who called him Sunny George, the only one of nine to see the other side of sixty-five. I witnessed an adult party at his mother Nana's house. I don't remember why I was there. Maybe I was at my cousin's next door and sneaked over into the kitchen to watch. Nana sang "Ain't She Sweet" with dramatic hand gestures. My Aunt Evelyn danced seductively with a feather boa. Uncle Bob recited a poem and Uncle Frankie told a joke. Only my father didn't perform.

He truly appreciated his good fortune and never forgot his roots. It was so much of his appeal. He was as comfortable drinking beer and playing pinochle with his brothers as he was sipping scotch and playing gin rummy at the club. He bridged both worlds with the help of my mother, who came from the other side of the tracks.

He made us feel special. His grand gestures included a day in the city to experience different modes of transportation. We boarded the Long Island Rail Road, taxied to the Pan Am Building for a ride in a helicopter and then cruised on the Circle Line tour boat around Manhattan. Another time we had lunch at the Palm Court at The Plaza to learn the art and etiquette of fine dining. One year the Christmas present for the five of us was a limo into the city for a day of beauty at

Elizabeth Arden's Red Door. I think my mother was behind these plans.

He was fun. A seasoned gin rummy player, he shuffled cards with flair and taught us rummy, solitaire and hearts. We learned the box step standing in our bare feet on top of his white buck shoes. Always a hit at the father daughter dances; he signed his notes to us, "Cha cha cha."

He made us feel protected. Not his usual genial self, he gave boys who came to call the third degree. Where are you taking my daughter? Whose car are you driving? Do you plan to go to college? When I asked him why he didn't act like himself with my dates, he explained that they were after something he wasn't anxious to give up.

He only raised his voice to us if we were being disrespectful to our mother. "Don't you talk to your mother that way." If we tried to explain ourselves beginning with she, he would cut us off with "She is a cat." He always gave our mother credit for all her work at Christmas and the wonderful care she lavished on him when he was sick. Her name was Betty, but he called her Jep. I recall my father bounding down the stairs one morning declaring, "Your mother was a tiger last night." We either ignored such comments or cried, "Daaady" I am sure my mother knew our father in ways we didn't.

One night when I was a teenager, he showed me his vulnerable side. I found him pacing the carpeted floor in the upstairs hallway walking back and forth in front of the table that held the rotary phone. I asked, "What's wrong, Dad?"

"I have to give a speech tonight and I can't do it" He was the chairman of a golf tournament at the Cherry Valley Country Club. He loved the game and the men he played with.

"Why not?"

"I can't talk in front of a group of people. I'll just freeze." Dad called a friend, said he was sick and that week he signed up for a Dale Carnegie course. He lacked the education and background of his friends. He never denied his roots, which were part of his charm, but there were times that he felt inadequate.

He never discussed money with us. It was considered impolite conversation. There was no talk about any of his daughters entering his company. He did let me do some paperwork occasionally, which made me feel very important. I dreamed of being president of Lane Office Furniture.

After high school my sisters and I all went away--away being the operative word--to some type of school: secretarial, junior college, college. Not so much for the degree, but for the exposure. We were expected to meet and marry men who would take care of us. Since I was the only one who attended a four-year college, my father encouraged me to become a teacher as an insurance policy in case, god forbid, my husband should die.

So I had big expectations for my first husband Jack, which wasn't entirely fair. At first, I was idealistic and into a hippie phase when I thought material things didn't matter. Easy for a pampered girl to think. Plus the pedestal I had placed him on was doomed to fall.

After my parents gave us $9,000, half of the money we needed to buy our first house in Hampton Bays, Jack didn't work that summer--not to stay home and help me with two babies but because he felt it was demeaning for a teacher to have a summer job. Not having enough money to buy a magazine wore thin.

Money became a big issue. Although we had agreed that I wouldn't go back to teaching until our two children were in school, I never felt that Jack valued me unless I was contributing a paycheck.

We accepted money and gifts from my generous parents that enabled us to live a grander life than our salaries allowed. I thanked my parents for offering to pay our children's college tuition, but I felt it was our responsibility. I wish my husband had been the one to make that decision. At home I was the disciplinarian, telling my daughter, "Don't you talk to your father like that." Our roles seemed reversed, and I didn't like it.

Although my father said that the women's lib thing was going to backfire, work was my salvation. It was where I felt most like myself. My job also enabled me to leave an unfulfilling marriage and provide for myself. In those years I made peace with money.

I remarried in 2001. Terry tells me he is sorry he never met my father because people have told him countless times, "We loved Denise's parents, especially her father. George was such a great guy." I look for hints of my father in my husband that I know I will find. He makes me laugh, he opens doors for me and holds my hand, he makes me feel special, and I let him see the vulnerable side of me.

❖❖❖❖❖

I look down from the bridge and see that someone has drawn a large heart in wet sand left by the receding tide. Mentally I fill in the center with the letters—D A D D Y.

Span 10

Stairs

The white caps on Shinnecock Bay stampede in front of the west wind. I walk by the beach to the left of the bridge and examine low tides' expose`. Unearthed pilings cast a shadow on the wet sand that looks like a staircase. I think back to the ones in the houses where I grew up.

Coming back from the city recently, I decided to drive by my old neighborhood. I made a left off Northern Boulevard onto Nassau Road where I lived from age five to sixteen. I rolled to a stop in front of #67. The front yard where we ran under the diamond dots of the sprinkler in the summer, raked piles of yellow and red leaves in the fall, rolled the body parts of a snowman in the winter, and hid Easter eggs in the spring seemed the size of a postage stamp.

Sitting in my car I pictured the house as I remembered it. The center hallway was like the spoke of a wheel with rooms radiating off it, as well as the staircase to the children's rooms on the second floor

The staircase I raced down as fast as a speeding bullet to see if I could fly. I crashed often and remember my father running out of the bathroom with a wash cloth in front of his privates furious at me.

The staircase the five of us assembled, youngest first, on Christmas morning, dressed in matching red pajamas, in slippered feet and wrapped in tartan plaid robes, to be dazzled by a tree with colored lights, tinsel, glass ornaments, and Styrofoam balls intricately pinned with sequins on snowy days. A tree that hadn't been there the night before and piles of presents we had dreamed about that sleepless night while butterflies danced in our stomachs.

The staircase my father bounded up to tell us a story and kiss us good night. His tales always revolved around a poor boy who was deeply in love with the princess with no hope of winning her hand. One day the king proclaimed that whoever presented his daughter with the most beautiful dress in all the land would be her prince. The boy wandered into the woods and cried. His tears turned into crystals and his friends, the creatures of the woods, surrounded him. My father would go on in detail how they helped him with their webs, feathers, and gifts of the forest to create a dress so magical the princess instantly fell in love with him, and they lived happily ever after.

The staircase we descended oldest first for an Easter morning fashion show. My father, behind the blinding Super 8 moving camera lights, directed and commentated "and here is Denise looking terrific in a red coat and HIGH HEELS. Suzan is wearing a pillbox with a veil and hanging purple flowers. Oh la la. Lovely Laura is modeling her dress and showing us all those petticoats. Jenny's wearing a pale blue suit with white gloves carrying a pocketbook that matches her hat. Pam looks so pretty in her straw hat and shiny patent leather shoes.

The staircase I marched down proudly in my Saint Mary's uniform the first day of high school. White starched shirt under a navy blazer, grey gore shaped skirt just below the knee and brand new black and white saddle shoes and bobby socks. Fast forward to sophomore year only the collar and front placket of my shirt are ironed, the skirt is rolled at the waist before and after school, and a student council armband is branded on my blazer like a tattoo.

The staircase where I sat on the bottom step waiting for the phone to ring. Our only phone was above a radiator that was enclosed in a painted white cabinet in the center hall. The cord on the phone was long enough to stretch into my parents' bedroom where I could close the door for privacy.

The staircase I skipped down with sweaty palms on the first date that really counted. Afterwards awkward sweet kisses. Two years later I waltzed down the stairs in my red and white gingham checked spaghetti-strapped dress for his junior prom. At the end of the night, our bodies were entwined like the honeysuckle vine that covered the trellis by the kitchen door

A grander staircase came into my life the summer before my senior year in 1962 when we moved further east on the south shore to a house in Garden City. It had an additional flight of stairs that led up to the third floor, which I shared with Suzan. The landing was a large square carpeted area big enough to stretch out on the floor and talk on the phone for hours.

One September day in 1963, I walked down those stairs and left for college. Before my parents and I were out of the driveway heading for Philadelphia, Laura was moving into my domain.

I had already said goodbye to my boyfriend, but he was still parked outside the house. He drove his father's Oldsmobile up next to my father's Cadillac. We held hands through the open windows, until we turned and he went in the other direction.

Four years later as a June bride, I glided down those stairs in my wedding gown towards my father who would give me away.

When the honeymoon was over, my husband and I rented a garden apartment for two years. Two babies later we lived in a small ranch in a town where my family had spent their summers.

It had no stairs.

Nest

Ospreys return to the same nest, adding to it year after year. The home on Dune Road near the Shinnecock Bridge had to be rebuilt after Super Storm Sandy, so it's fairly modest. The outside is composed of small branches and twigs, but the inside is lined for breeding with leaves and feathers. I leave hair clippings and corn silk on the deck and imagine them being woven into luxurious bedding. My nest is important to me, but I haven't always feathered it.

After we secured teaching jobs on Long Island, Jack, my fiancé, wanted to buy a house in a Levitt development with the insurance money from a car accident. During spring break of my senior year, we looked at decorated models in Stony Brook. I halfheartedly picked my favorite. I was more focused on finals and kissing my college life goodbye

It's not that I didn't love Jack, the first guy I slept with, I just really didn't care about getting married. I had hoped that I would meet my future husband before graduation, and tie the knot down the road. But Jack, four years older than me, knew what he wanted and that included a family before he turned thirty.

After I admitted that a house seemed like a commitment I wasn't ready for, we talked about a fabulous honeymoon instead. My mother encouraged us saying that we would eventually have a house, but a four-week trip to Europe might be a once in a lifetime opportunity. That dream holiday got me through piles of dirty diapers and lean times.

My first married home was a garden apartment in Nesconset where the bedroom and dining area were each filled with a suite of Ethan Allen Early American furniture, wedding gifts from our parents. We bought a small couch and a round coffee table to complete our furnishings. Jack presented me with sterling silver place settings for twelve as a wedding gift and Havilland china from his grandmother. Those things mattered to him. I wasn't ready to be Susie homemaker.

It was in this apartment that I learned some of the realities of money. Armed with a list for my first food shopping excursion, I innocently added a few items that tempted me. When I checked out, the bill was $15 more than our food budget, so I left the meat behind because the math was easier. Jack was incredulous and informed me that there was no more money, so we had a meatless week. I found it hard to fathom that the couple who lived next door to us, Alice and Ralph Kramden knockoffs, made more money than we did. In 1967 our combined income as teachers was about $13,000.

By the end of our two-year lease, we had a daughter, and I was pregnant with our son. Jack thought it was a waste of money to continue paying rent; he wanted a house. I knew we would need more space. We could no longer afford the development we initially liked. To find a place in our price range we had to look out east, which meant a longer commute to work for Jack and later for me. We decided it was important for me to be a stay-at-home mom until both our children were in school.

Jack found a spec house, a small ranch, advertised in the New York Times for $18,000. It was in Hampton Bays, a community where I had spent my summers as a kid. I wanted to live at the beach or in the city, not in between in suburbia where I grew up. At the time I didn't appreciate the difference between a summer person and a local.

Our neighborhood was populated with State Troopers and their families. It was a safe place where doors were never locked and kids played outside. I loved the time with my children, but I was desperate for adult company. I was invited to the neighborhood coffee klatch, but sitting around talking about clipping coupons wasn't my cup of tea. I tried to organize the women to form a playgroup for our children. "Doesn't anybody want a few hours to themselves?" They didn't see the need.

As an advocate of women's lib, I suggested a consciousness-raising group. They weren't interested in Betty Friedan or Gloria Steinem. Their husbands certainly wouldn't like it. They were good people who thought I was a braless hippie. So I'd arrive late to their bingo games, drain the punch bowl and marvel at how one of the gals managed to feed her family on $40 a week.

Jack didn't bother much with the neighbors. He rarely accompanied me and the kids to the beach or other outings because he was coaching, smoking his pipe in his wood-paneled office in the back of our one-car garage or he just didn't feel like it. Word around town was that I was a widow.

In those early years I went into decorator mode, so beautifully modeled by my mother, to transform our house into a home. I wallpapered my daughter Melissa's room in red and white check, draped the windows with dotted Swiss curtains and hung large posters of Beatrix Potter figures. My son Ashley's room was yellow and white with a brown giraffe motif. I found a lone star quilt for our bed that picked up the green and blue of a set of prints we had bought on our honeymoon. The love seat from our apartment was replaced by two blue and pink floral slipcovered couches from my mother's house. I needlepointed four large squares in a geometric print to grace the walls. A set of embroidered and framed spice samplers hung in the blue and white kitchen.

Just before both my children would be standing together for the first time at the bus stop in September, I was offered a job. The position was for a Title 1 reading teacher at Hampton Bays Junior Senior High School. My daughter's teacher had recommended me. Most sane women would have been popping the champagne corks when their youngest started school, but I bought into the superwoman role. I jumped on that job offer like it was the last bus home.

It was convenient to work in Hampton Bays. I was able to usher my kids out the door to catch the school bus, straighten the house and throw a load of laundry into the washing machine before I left for work. But after several years I reached a point where I felt like I knew everyone in town and more of their business than I cared to know. It was also difficult to be a private citizen. I thought twice before going to the supermarket with a raincoat over my pajamas since the chances of an impromptu teacher conference with a parent were good.

One day driving home from the beach with my daughter and son, impulsively I turned right instead of left. Heading towards the dead end to the bay, I was drawn to a for sale sign nailed to a tree in front of a vacant lot. There was another car already parked there. The kids and I still in wet bathing suits and sandy feet got out of my VW bug to walk the property

By 1975 we had expanded our house as much as possible within the original footprint without building up. I was tired of it and the lack of privacy in our treeless development where everyone knew what you were barbequing for dinner. By then we had lived in our house for seven years, and I had an itch.

A blonde woman bustled toward me. I greeted her, "Hi. What a great spot."

"Yeah. I think so too. You know there are two lots here."

"Really?"

"I spoke to the owner, a local guy, yesterday."

"What's he asking?"

"$18,000 for the property bordering the road and $20,000 for the flag lot. I was hoping to negotiate, but his prices are firm."

"Which one are you interested in?"

"I really want the back lot. I think the water view from a second floor would be fabulous."

I nodded, "I'm going to climb a tree on the front piece to see if the water view I suspect is there." With a boost from my future neighbor, I found a foothole in the oak tree and reached up to the next branch thinking how I wanted, needed, to expand my world. Building a new house would provide a creative outlet. When I moved to a higher level, I was rewarded with a view that settled my soul and said you belong here.

Walking over to her, I extended my hand, "My name is Denise Helm; I think we're going to be neighbors."

"Mary Rooney. Good to meet you."

I drove home and told my husband about my discovery and that I knew it was meant to be. We had to buy it. We'd use our house as collateral and figure out the rest later. The rest was one bill that we couldn't cover, so I decided to change my job. The Title 1 position salary was paid on a per diem basis; I needed a tenure track teaching job with a contract and a pay scale. By 1975 my house and life felt claustrophobic; this new project provided an escape.

We met with my cousin Evelyn's husband, Johnny, who had designed my parent's summer place. I told him I wanted to make optimum use of the water view. I envisioned spacious living areas with lots of light. We couldn't waste money on rooms that were rarely used.

Before it was popular, Johnny planned a great room with a beamed cathedral ceiling on the second floor. Large Anderson windows framed an eastern and southern vista of Shinnecock Bay and on a rough day the Atlantic Ocean. The kitchen is tucked under one eave and an office and bathroom on the other with a stair case, fireplace and an entertainment center in between.

Downstairs he designed three bedrooms, two baths and a family room that faces south. In the winter the house is flooded with light, and thanks to the angle of the sun and the pitch of the roof, there is no direct sun in the summer.

Melissa was eight and Ashley seven when we moved into 52 Shinnecock Road. For the most part there were many happy memories in this house. I loved when the children came running into our bed at the first clap of thunder. The day after Thanksgiving we blasted Handel's Messiah daily for the rest of the season. We had magical Christmas mornings. We weren't the family that prayed together, but we did sit together for dinner most nights. No fast food. No television allowed.

But the predominate memories were parties. Jack was a good cook, and we entertained often. For years I lost Sunday morning to hangovers. When I ask my children about their memories in the house, to my dismay they mention all the parties they had when we weren't home. Our house was party central with the beach at the end of our street named after my daughter, "Melissa's Beach."

The empty nest was traumatic for me. I attended my daughter Melissa's high school graduation with wet hair. If I wasn't running to the store to buy more potato salad, a pound at a time, during her party, I was in the bathroom blowing into a paper bag to ward off a panic attack. My gift was a poem I had written entitled "Apron Strings." Our relationship during her teens had been a tug of war. When my son Ashley left for college two years later, I felt that the door to my life had closed behind him.

At that point I didn't know that they'd be back, and at some point, I would be begging them to leave. But I did see it as a make or break it time for couples. I wished I was giddy to find myself alone with my husband.

In the early 90s when we were trying to save a marriage mortared with more than twenty years of engrained habits, I wanted two things. The first was to have more family time and fun vacations. J World Sailing School in Key West, Florida, fit the bill. I had a great time with the children, but it didn't matter to me that Jack was with us.

The second thing I wanted was to decorate. Our unadorned house was filled with hand-me-downs from my parents. In all of our married years, we rarely bought our own furniture. But I came to realize that new furniture and trimmings wouldn't fill the void I felt in my marriage.

My mother said, "It's a bad sign when a woman stops feathering her nest." She was right. When Jack and I got divorced our agreement was simple. He didn't want me to touch his pension; I wanted the house.

I always felt it was mine.

Birth

From the couch I can see the head of a new day crowning on the horizon. It's my oldest grandson Riley's birthday. He's ten. It seems like he has been in my life forever. Being a grandmother has been an unexpected love affair.

My daughter Melissa's pregnancy had not been easy. She was in the hospital with high blood pressure the day of her baby shower. The morning Riley was born we were pushed out of Melissa's room when her blood pressure began to spike. I fought back the urge to scream, "Take the baby. Save my daughter." When it was all over, I threw myself on her bed and wept with relief.

My mother had died two months earlier that April. Melissa was having lunch with her when she collapsed and was taken to the hospital. The last time Melissa saw her grandmother, she placed her hands on Melissa's belly and felt the knobs and bumps of her first great-grandchild. Riley's birth filled some of the space my mother left.

During my morning walk, I thought about the day Melissa was born: September 28, 1968. After filling out the admission forms, my husband Jack came to the room to say good-bye. In those days husbands were excused from one of the most important events of their lives. He asked what I was doing as I grabbed the side rails and contorted my body. I explained that I was trying to get into a comfortable position, so the pain would go away. He informed me that wouldn't happen until the baby was born. I felt indignant.

Chain-smoking and talking on the phone helped pass the endless hours. At one point I was given an enema and the nurse repeated. "Hold. Hold." Then she said, "Okay, you can go now," and I did. The heavyset nurse yelled, "What are you doing? Not in the bed." I was mortified; I had no clue. When I asked my mother why she didn't tell me what to expect, she explained she didn't want to scare me.

There had been a serious car accident nearby that day, which meant emergency surgeries. No anesthesiologist was available, so the birth was natural. The back pain felt like I was going to have a bowel movement the size of a watermelon that would split me in two. When my daughter was born, she could have been a gorilla. All I cared about was that the pain was gone.

After being polite for 24 hours, when I felt the prick of a needle I sat up and screamed, "If you think I am going to lie here while you stitch me up..." Before I could finish, I was assured that what I felt was a shot of Novocain. The nurse told me to roll on my stomach onto the gurney. Exhausted I snapped, "I can't. I am nine months pregnant."

Back in the room my tiny rosebud daughter, swaddled in a pink blanket and cap was placed in the crook of my arm. An older no-nonsense nurse asked me if I was planning to nurse. Before I had the word 'yes' out of my mouth, she had latched Melissa to my breast. The miracle dawned on me. I am a mother. I gave her life; she would give me the meaning of the word joy.

❖❖❖❖❖

In the Ponquogue parking lot I notice stubby green grass pushing through the macadam in crooked lines. New snow fencing snakes through the fragile dunes. The raw brown newness of the pine slats connected to the weathered grey ones.

The Unlocking

This February has been arctic with record-breaking cold. Peconic Bay was sealed in and ice boats scraped across "the hard water" on Mecox and the Great South Bay. Along the whitewashed Shinnecock shores the ripple of waves froze in motion as chunks of ice choked the channels and clumped onto the beach.

I tried to take a walk last week, but it was too cold and windy. Instead I drove across the bridge and into the ocean parking lot where I passed seagulls sitting in a circle while a sole tern scurried around the outside of the flock. I wished one of the gulls would have lifted her wing and sheltered the lost bird.

❖❖❖❖❖

Suzan and I had just settled on the couch with a glass of wine when her phone rang. Damn. It's impossible to have an uninterrupted conversation with my sister. She and I are thirteen months apart and have always been close, but since she moved to Florida our in-person visits are rare. She looked up at me and mouthed, "It's Chris." Her son-in-law. And from her expression I knew that there was something wrong with her daughter, Sarah. "Sarah's in the hospital. They think it's her appendix."

"Oh dear. What are you thinking?"

"I guess I better check flights."

Sitting on the edge of the bed in the guest room while she packed her suitcase, I told her how disappointed I was that our infrequent visit was being cut short. She was leaving for Texas early the next morning. Part of me felt jealous that this mother would drop everything and travel across country to be with her daughter. It triggered something visceral, and I experienced waves of self-pity. When she started to talk about what kind of scar Sarah might have, I wanted to whip down my pants and say, "Take a look at mine."

Feelings, stitched into the four-inch scar stretched years ago by my pregnant belly and indented where a drainage tube had resided, began to surface. I felt overwhelmingly sad.

When my alarm went off the next morning, I got up to make sure my sister was awake. She was dressed and ready to go. The bed was made, the room neat and tidy like her. Then she was gone. Drained of energy, I spent the day in bed remembering.

❖❖❖❖❖

The day her first grandchild was born, my mother arrived at the hospital with boxes and boxes of presents tied with pink ribbons from Lord & Taylor. She returned to help me after I brought my little miss home. I was feeling good, and anxious to take on my new role as a mother, I probably didn't take advantage of my mother being there. I can envision her polishing apples from a bowl on the dining room table before she left.

❖❖❖❖❖

Six weeks after my daughter was born in 1968, I was hospitalized with a pain that doubled me over. During the intake at Smithtown General Hospital, I was asked if I had had sex before the prescribed waiting period. I had. So for two weeks I was treated for what they thought was a pelvic infection. The following year, it would be determined that I had had a ruptured appendix. I remember being told I was delirious with a high fever lying on a bed in an alcove until a room became available. I remember keeping a picture of my baby daughter under my pillow. I remember my hospital roommate, a teenager who had been expelled from high school for attacking another student. She had a broken leg in traction, the TV on 24-7 and no visitors. I felt sorry for her because she didn't seem to have anyone.

During the two weeks I was in the hospital, only my husband was a regular visitor. My father and two of my four younger sisters came to see me, but just once. My mother never came.

My parents and sisters, who lived an hour away, took care of my daughter for the first week until a virus jumped from one family member to another. Then my husband and a neighbor we barely knew took the following week.

Missing my daughter terribly, I showed her picture to every doctor, nurse, orderly, and volunteer who entered the room. I had been nursing her, but I was too sick to pump my breasts while in the hospital. My fear was that she would feel abandoned and forget me.

After I was discharged I went directly to my neighbor's apartment to claim my child. When I saw how my tiny baby had plumped up and grown without me, I cried. She smiled up at me, and I smothered her with kisses.

My husband opened the door to our curtainless apartment that smelled like he had sprayed furniture polish as a room freshener. I was weak and a bit unsteady. Except for baby formula, a few bottles of beer, and a grease-stained Chinese takeout box, the refrigerator was empty.

No one was there to help me. I was 22, which meant my youngest sisters were in high school, one was away at college and the other was working. Where was my mother?

❖❖❖❖❖

I never thought of myself as being alone. There were five of us in seven years. Growing up in a large family, being part of a litter, we were rarely by ourselves. Throughout my life I have been blessed with friends, but after four years of college in Philadelphia, the high school group had scattered like the seeds of a dandelion, and my college friends were rooted out of state. My husband and I had moved into a garden apartment complex near Smithtown after we were married. We had both gotten teaching jobs nearby. I was pregnant by the end of the school year. Other than chatting with our next door neighbors, we hadn't established a circle of friends yet. Still on a honeymoon with my husband and so in love with my first baby who was born that September, I hadn't noticed I was alone.

❖❖❖❖❖

A year later, six months pregnant with my second baby and newly settled in Hampton Bays, I woke up with a burning in my gut. "Don't go to work today." I told my husband, "I have that pain again. I need to go to the hospital." Thinking I was experiencing false labor, the admitting doctor at Southampton Hospital wanted to send me home. "I'm not leaving. I know I'm sick, I'm really sick."

The next morning, after a series of tests, the doctor stood in the doorway of my hospital room. "Denise, we are going to operate today." I don't remember much else after that. It was the day of my sister Suzan's wedding. I pulled the sheet up over my face and wept. I thought I was going to die along with my unborn child, and I was leaving my daughter motherless with no chance to say good bye. I didn't want to call my family and upset them. They knew I had been hospitalized and weren't expecting us at the wedding. My husband, a high school teacher and football coach had an away game. I couldn't get in touch with him because there were no answering machines or cell phones in the late '60s.

After the surgery my doctor reported that I probably had had a ruptured appendix the previous year. Because of all the medication that I had received, the infection had been localized. A year later, an abscess had formed in the area causing the pain. I returned home to my fourteen-month-old baby, who I wasn't supposed to lift. My husband worked all day and didn't do much when he was home. No one came to help me.

❖❖❖❖❖

Now, I ask myself where my mother was, but at the time I assumed whatever she did or didn't do was normal. Like my mother, I am the first born. I didn't ask for help, so maybe she didn't think I needed it. That became a pattern in my life.

When I was newly divorced, on my own for the first time in twenty-five years, I won a National Endowment for the Humanities to study at University of North Carolina's Summer Seminar. It was an intellectual and emotional giant step for me. The night before I was leaving, my mother mentioned she was concerned about the weather. It was supposed to rain heavily the next day and my youngest sister Pam was having a yard sale. "Mom, not for nothing, but tomorrow I will be driving to North Carolina by myself in the rain."

"Oh, you'll be fine. I don't have to worry about you.

❖❖❖❖❖

I was concerned about how the operation would affect the baby I was carrying. The doctor had assured me that my baby would be fine, unharmed by the procedure. But when he was born three months later, he wasn't fine.

After I heard his newborn cry, the room filled with a deafening silence; I knew something was wrong. My son was born with a bilateral cleft lip and palette.

He was transferred to North Shore Hospital where he would have his first operation after he reached ten pounds. We stayed with my family who lived nearby.

When we returned to our house in Hampton Bays, my mother hired a local woman, "Aunt Grace," to help with my seventeen-month-old daughter a few hours a week. She was a British war bride and entertained me with stories, but she wasn't my mother.

❖❖❖❖❖

My mother disappeared; my father made magic. Before my mother had her driving license, we would all pile into my father's Buick and head for Mays or Lanes department stores. The five of us would sit in the back seat, steaming up the windows while we waited in the parking lot. She and my father had probably agreed on a time. Five minutes before that hour, he would incant an elaborate magical spell ending with "a bra ca dab ra open sesame," and our mother would walk through the doors laden with shopping bags.

My mother's absences were a mystery to us. It bothered my sister Jennifer that our mother would come home after months in Florida, the day after a grandchild's first Holy Communion or Confirmation or dance recital. "All Mommy's friends were at their grandchildren's functions. Where was she?"

❖❖❖❖❖

The New Years Eve before my son's first birthday and his second operation, my mother embraced me crying, "I don't know how you have handled this. I don't know how you do it…the difficult feedings, the operations, the speech therapy." I was so angry, I walked away. I wanted to scream, "Why couldn't you feed your grandson?" "Why couldn't you say the things I need to hear when you are sober?" "Why did you wait so long to say anything?"

Those feelings had no words; if they had words, there was no voice. If I had a voice, there was no audience. My emotional hieroglyphics were iced in crystal patterns and I skated through life on blades of denial and stoicism.

❖❖❖❖❖

In my forties when my marriage was crumbling, I went into therapy. I don't recall what I said, but the well dressed therapist's question and my responses were what were important. Stroking his neatly groomed beard he asked, "How did you feel about ....?"

"Well I thought that"

"No, How did you feel when....?"

"I imagined that ...."

"No." He stopped me mid-sentence. "How did you feel?"

"I considered that"

He stretched out his thin fingers on his pressed pant legs and leaned forward, "No, Denise. You are giving me thinking responses. How did you feel?"

I stared into his eyes, scanned the walls of his credentials, and glanced at magazine covers looking for a clue. It surprised me that he hadn't raised his voice each time asking the same question, like people sometimes do when they are speaking to foreigners. I snapped back, "What am I supposed to say?" I don't get what you want. Give me a script."

And then my education in expressing feelings began with a vocabulary lesson.

❖❖❖❖❖

Looking back, it seems that my mother didn't talk a lot. Really talk, not just the daily-dos. I don't think it was just talking to me that made her uncomfortable. My sisters wished that she had given them advice or direction when they felt lost. Once when I approached her with something that was bothering me she snapped, "I can't solve the problems of five daughters."

"Mom, I don't expect you to, I just want you to listen." But then she would become busier cleaning up the kitchen or rushing because she was late. She never sat down, had a cup of tea, and really focused on me.

I wondered about her mother, Grammy, who later in life was a businesswoman and worked at her husband's real estate office. I loved her long bony fingers that danced across the piano keys, cut the crusts off our Wonder Bread sandwiches, taught us how to knit and crochet and most of all tickled my back. My sister Pam once mentioned that Grammy never told us that she loved us. I was shocked; I never noticed. As the first grandchild, I knew I was special and assumed she had said the magic words. Did my mother think her mother's lack of verbal affection was normal?

❖❖❖❖❖

When I was divorced in my forties, I rented my house and used my mother's summer home as a base camp. I don't know if my mother had a drinking problem when she was younger, but she did in her older years. One night, after what my adult children called "the witching hour," Mom, fortified with drink, stated, "I think you were better off married. He would take you back. Once you get a little older, things don't matter so much."

I verbally jacked her up against the wall and seethed, "Mom, I just need you to tell me that everything is going to be fine."

My mother had things she wanted to say, but unless she was drinking she didn't, couldn't. At night she would go into her bedroom and have conversations with herself and make noises that made me want to escape into another part of the house and close the door. I wished I had gone into her room, held her and whispered, "Mom, everything is going to be fine."

When she was dying the hospice nurses encouraged us to tell her to let go, to give her permission to die; that we would be okay. I had said the same things to my father four years earlier. Although I felt closer to him, I had a terrible time letting my mother go. There was a part of me that would have kept her in a coma, rather than to have her disappear from me forever.

❖❖❖❖❖

After my niece recovered from her surgery, I decided to send my sisters a group email and explain that my godchild's appendectomy had resurrected this ancient history. I didn't want to blame them. They were young and my mother hadn't set the example, but I wanted them to know. I needed witnesses to that part of my life. They responded just the way I hoped they would. "I had no idea; I am sorry you were so alone; I wish I had been there for you; it must have been terribly hard." And like the month of March, the unlocking of those feelings began. The ice cracked and heaved and broke away and began to thaw.

❖❖❖❖❖

The seascape is ghostly white like the skin on top of scalded milk. Standing at the slush line with my binoculars I focus on a dark spot out on the water and realize that it is a tight ring of birds, like a wagon train forming a circle.

Friday the 13th

My waking thought is today's my son Ashley's 40th birthday. The movie of that day starts playing in my mind as I head for the beach. The 15 to 20 mile an hour wind calls for a different route. I park at the beach and walk towards the underside of the bridge. The tall cattails bow in the wind sweeping across goldenrod, grey barberry and ripening vines.

The underside of the bridge with its oversized cement legs and center arches stands solid and strong. Silent with captured grey light stolen from the sun, I feel an ethereal presence like looking through a Greek Temple. It evoked prayer. I bend my head in gratitude for my son and the wonderful man he has become.

Ashley was born on his due date Friday the 13th, 1970. The superstitious day had always been lucky for me. I took it as a good omen. After spending 24 hours alone in the hospital when my daughter, Melissa, was born, I was determined not to have the same experience. Mild contractions started during the night. I told my husband to go to work; I would call him. It wasn't until about 9 a.m. that I decided to report to my obstetrician. The bearable contractions were five minutes apart. The nurse told me to come right in.

By the time I packed and dropped my daughter at a neighbor's house, it was close to 10. The seat in my VW bug was pushed back as far as it could go to accommodate my pregnant belly and still close enough to reach the pedals. As I shifted into fourth gear on Montauk Highway, I realized that the contractions were serious. Fortunately, the doctor's office was only twenty minutes away. The nurse at reception took one look at me and led me to an examining room.

I lay on the white-paper-covered table, rested my feet in the stirrups and began to count the holes in the acoustical ceiling. My favorite, Doctor Johnson, walked through the door, gloves ready. After a quick look "down there," he announced, "Denise, this baby isn't going to wait much longer."

I grasped his hand, "No. No. I'm not ready." I had not forgotten the pain that they say you will forget from my first delivery.

"Dr. Halsey is leaving for the hospital. He'll take you in his car."

A Jimmy Stewart lookalike, he never said much. He didn't say much when my water broke in his car. In the hospital, bent over in pain with each article of clothing I removed, I knew I didn't have time to waste. On the gurney I was offered whiffs of gas that I sucked greedily and then blackness.

When I woke up I heard the lusty cry of a newborn. "I hear my baby, my baby. Boy or girl?"

"A boy."

I was rejoicing, thanking God for a son since we already had a daughter, when the stillness started to seep into my consciousness and creep into the pit of my stomach. I heard the wall of silence. The drip drip drip of a faucet, the clang of metal instruments. "What's wrong?"

"The baby has a birth defect," the doctor replied.

"What kind?"

"A bilateral cleft lip and palate."

I envisioned people I had seen with a harelip. "How bad is it?"

There was a long pause. "It's severe."

"Would you like to see him?" asked the nurse.

"I'm afraid."

"You don't have to now."

"No, that would be like rejecting him." And she placed my swaddled son into my arms, a round eight pounds nine ounces. The middle of his lip and gum was rolled up under his nose, and there was no floor to his left nostril. My immediate concern was that he was in pain. I kissed his forehead.

I think it's safe to say that every expectant mother worries about the health of the baby she is carrying. Today, I imagine there are few surprises. In 1970 there were no sonograms of babies in utero looking like floating aliens. There was no battery of tests.

My greatest fear was to have a mentally handicapped child. Down syndrome children were more prevalent in those days usually born to older parents. I was only 23, yet I worried. Call it religious superstition or Irish premonition, I always knew I would have a child with a problem. We had been taught that everyone had a cross to bear. My life had been charmed, so I expected this. I was relieved; I could handle a physical problem that could be repaired.

I heard footsteps running down the hall. Dr. Johnson rushed to me, sat on the bed, held my hand and told me everything would be all right. He had had a college roommate with the same problem. It could be taken care of. Doctor Halsey had shrugged his shoulders and said he wasn't sure where we should go. Jack arrived with news that my parents had contacted doctor friends who could help us. He was strong; I would be too.

My family connected us to Doctor Walden, the head of the Cleft Lip and Palate Center at North Shore Hospital, in Manhasset. We stayed at my parents' home since we lived 60 miles away. My family babysat for our toddler, Melissa, while I practically lived in the hospital. Although they were very helpful, no one talked about my son's condition; nobody cried. I got the message to be strong. I wasn't until years later that I learned that my mother had been distraught.

When my son was ten pounds, he had his first operation. Although his father and I stood by his metal crib thinking he would die, neither of us said anything. A young priest appeared and wondered if we wanted our child to be baptized, which confirmed my fears. When father asked the name, I answered," Ashley Sloan Helm." He replied that since that probably wasn't a saint's name, he would baptize my son John. I thanked him, told him that I would do it myself, and turned my back on him. An hour later a seasoned priest stood in the doorway and asked if he could help. I repeated the name and he agreed to baptize him.

Ashley's condition would require at least half a dozen surgeries, countless doctor appointments and speech therapy twice a week for years at North Shore Hospital, a three hour round-trip drive. In order to cope, I only worried about immediate concerns. The long term overwhelmed me. I knew I couldn't break down, so I basically shut down. It was easier to deny feelings, and I certainly wasn't going to talk about them.

During the early hospital stays we were often surrounded by very ill children, which reinforced how selfish it would be to be sad. The bottom line was that I was terrified that if I let myself lose it, I'd never come back. So I sobbed during TV commercials, wailed at movies, whimpered during the National Anthem. A friend called it misplaced tears. My car and the shower were my cryatoriums where I would sob for no apparent reason at times when my life was breezing along.

On February 4, 2006, our third grand boy, a little peanut with big eyes, was born three weeks early. Jeremy is my stepson David's first child, and we were thrilled. But I was unprepared at how much history came hurling back at me. When Stacy, my daughter-in-law, told me that they had put her baby in an isolette because he was jaundiced, I remembered that the kind nurses moved Ashley from the viewing window, so visitors wouldn't gawk at his deformity. Stacy was upset when Jeremy had to stay an extra day in the hospital. I wanted to say that Ashley spent his first two weeks in the pediatric ward.

At home she laughed that Jeremy seemed to be permanently connected to her breast. Ashley couldn't nurse because he had no roof to his mouth and had to be fed every two hours with a bulb syringe. Stacy used supplemental bottles, so David could help with the feeding. No one but me fed my son for the first three months. Not his father. Not my mother. They were afraid. Eventually with the use of a plastic prosthesis that I glued to his gums with denture powder, he was able to drink from a bottle.

Of course I don't burden her with my experiences. This is her first baby and a special time. It is her turn to tell stories about her son.

❖ ❖ ❖ ❖ ❖

It was the year Ashley turned twenty-one. His father and I had been pedaling past the farms on the North Fork of Long Island when the words to a still unfinished poem floated into my mind. "On an apple crisp September morn, I thought about the day my son was born and I cried." The floodgates opened and from Riverhead to Orient, I released old salty tears for myself and my imperfect baby, no longer afraid to let go.

Gone Fishing

From the Ponquogue Bridge, I see paddleboards like lily pads in the bay. The class members on their knees, hands in prayer position, bow in Namaste. On the floating dock below, a sole fisherman sits on an orange spackle bucket.

It brought to mind a "Gone Fishing" sign I saw as a young girl walking with my cousin Hedy. It hung from the rectory door of a white clapboard Protestant church. I remember thinking, how could he do that, close on a Sunday? But then as a Catholic, we had been taught that Protestants couldn't get into heaven, so it probably didn't matter.

On other Sundays, I would spot the minister after services standing outside the church greeting his flock. The Protestants always seemed more relaxed and friendly. They had strawberry festivals and summer barbeques, which really appealed to me, but they were not the chosen people.

I haven't been a practicing Catholic for decades, but if you were raised in my generation, the first wave of baby boomers, it's part of your DNA. My maternal grandmother, Grammy, was an unflinching believer. The three rosaries she recited daily served as an umbrella policy for the family.

When she died, I asked for a pair of her rosary beads. Expecting the black plastic ones, I was given the sterling silver beads she probably never took out of the felt pouch. I used to keep them in my car and pray while I was driving, until one day they got caught in the steering wheel column. My sister was having an operation that day. I thought for sure she was doomed.

My parents weren't religious, but my father drove us to the children's mass on Sunday morning. If we were late, we went to the mass in the cafeteria. He sat with his arms folded across his chest and slept. I remember nudging him once. He leaned down in his camel hair coat and whispered that he was just resting his eyes. hMy father told me later in life that he didn't believe in God. At his wake, I wanted to rip the rosary beads out of his hands and replace them with his putter.

My mother's beliefs were different. Leaving a trail of Arpege, she flew out of the house five minutes before the one o'clock mass. If she didn't find a good parking spot, she'd go to the movies. But to this day I can picture my mother kneeling at the foot of her bed praying.

In the 1950s we attended Saint Anastasia Grammar School in Little Neck where we memorized the Baltimore Catechism. There we learned the Ten Commandments. Questions about coveting thy neighbor's wife were never entertained, since questions in general were not allowed. The incomprehensible tenets of the Blessed Trinity, a god with multiple personalities, and a virgin mother among other mysteries were not to be challenged. We were told they were matters of faith.

Attendance at church on Sundays and Holy Days of Obligation was serious business. There were fasting and abstinence laws, that sometimes resulted in fainting or lightheadedness, which contributed to the otherworldly feeling, with organ music vibrating through your body and incense filling your head. That was the part I liked.

Almost everyone I knew went to a Catholic high school. At Saint Mary's I led my homeroom in daily recitation of the rosary in less than five minutes. I was president of the Legion of Mary. In church the girls sat on the left side of the aisle in front of her statue. Ave Maria was played at our weddings and my mother's funeral.

In my day there were two kinds of women: Mary, the Blessed Mother and Mary Magdalene, the fallen woman, which left a lot of people unaccounted for. It seemed to me that the church set teenagers up to fail. Confession was heard on Saturday afternoon followed by date night, which usually resulted in sin that could hardly be avoided since even thoughts or omissions were offenses. This meant you couldn't receive communion at Sunday mass. Everyone knew you had sinned, as they stepped over you in the pew on their way to receiving the thin white communion wafer that stuck to the roof of your mouth.

Birth control was a big issue. The rhythm method, approved by the church, worked if you were good with math and self-control. My mother had five girls in seven years. Lack of effective contraception led to unwanted pregnancies and abortions. Fortunately, I never had to make that decision, but I believe it is a woman's right to choose. The church disagrees.

Two weeks after graduation, I was married. Our parish priests' sermons were so simple-minded that I found myself wanting to stand up and scream. After being taught in college by the Sisters of Saint Joseph, who were worldly and educated, the discrimination of woman in the church was apparent to me. By the time my children were school age, Catholic school was not a consideration.

Even though my beliefs were like a fishnet, my children were baptized, and I attended mass with them when they were young. They both made their first Holy Communion, but hypocrisy haunted me. Divorce was a choice I made later in my life. It is not accepted by the church, but if you could afford it, annulments were an option. Catholic lite had worn thin; I drifted away. The term fallen away Catholic is a misnomer because falling suggests something immediate, when actually it's more like a chipping away.

When I was in Italy with three girlfriends before I remarried in 2001, we boarded a bus to Lucca, a walled town in Tuscany. When bells tolled from the church in the town square, we were drawn into the darkness of the ancient building. My friends walked in, genuflected and attended mass. I stood in the rear of the duoma, my back against the cool stone, and wept for that unshakeable faith I never had.

For years I just drifted along dragging my soul behind me. I don't believe in heaven or hell. I worried about what would comfort me after my parents died. The true believers have something to cling to in their grief. I had nothing, and it scared the hell out of me.

When I became an Adult Literacy tutor, my first student was a man named Frezell Stanley. I helped him earn his GED; he helped me to understand spirituality. One day he handed me *Blessed Are the Addicts*. I told him that I didn't want to read it because it was religious. He explained it was not religious but spiritual. I said, "Same thing."

"He countered, "Not really."

And thus the teacher became the student. I waded through books like *The Road Less Traveled* and *Born into the Light,* trying to fill a gaping hole. Like the snowy white egret stirring the sand with her feet, her toothpick beak ready, patiently waiting, I took what worked for me.

I believe in the soul, a higher power, the serenity prayer. I believe in the power of the mind, the miracle of love, and the golden rule. I practice meditation and yoga. And on Sunday mornings, I walk the Ponquogue Bridge.

Signs

The sky is finger-painted blue with thumb print clouds. A Suffolk County Public Works truck is parked half way up the Ponquogue Bridge. One guy is in the bucket, the other with a smiling face greets me.

"What a great day."

"It sure is. What's up?"

"We're changing a bulb."

"Again."

"Yeah and these bulbs aren't cheap, $300 a pop."

"Wow. That's crazy. How come they burn out so fast?"

"The wind, pardon my French, knocks the crap out of the batteries."

"How about the one light that comes on during the day?

"I don't know. Could be the wind there too."

I decide not to tell him my theory.

I believe that when we die, our love remains on earth, and our souls live on in the form of energy. I know and envy people who find absolute comfort in the thought of going to heaven. I just don't believe it. It's too confusing to think of all those first and second wives, former loves and exs living in harmony. Nor can I believe in hell where you burn for eternity, just because you didn't get around to confessing a mortal sin.

When I was ten, I had a tooth extracted. The nurse lowered the powdered rubber mask over my face and the sweet smell of ether took over. I dreamt that I was sucked into the darkness of death. I was in a breathless tunnel running toward the light to warn others not to die. This didn't help my belief in heaven, and if I didn't go to heaven was I bad enough to be in the other place. But much later in my life after reading *Embraced by the Light* about near death experiences, I realized that I had had it backwards.

Triggered by the fact that my friend Kathy Bodkin had lost both her parents and her in-laws within six months of each other, I started to deal with the reality of my parents' mortality. In their seventies their youthful mentalities remained, but the telltales signs of aging became hard to ignore. I was desperate to find something to believe in before they died, something that would fill the chasm left by my childhood religion, something that would help me in my grief.

One night at book group, clustered around Kathy's polished kitchen table, she spoke about signs she had received from her parents. Other friends chimed in with similar experiences from their departed love ones. They gave me hope.

I shared these accounts with my friend Alice, a science-based Episcopalian. She pretended to listen to them, kind of how a person who really doesn't like animals, tolerates people's pets' tales.

Alice does everything fast. When we were on vacation together before my eyelids were open, hers were lined with black eyeliner. At dinner, she's always the first with a happy plate. So it's not surprising that she collects rabbit figurines, statues and paintings.

Her oldest sister, Dell, was as slow as Alice is speedy. If Alice's totem is a rabbit, Dell's was a turtle. On a cruel March morning Alice stood on the front lawn watching the men from the funeral pallor wheel her sister's body toward the hearse parked in the driveway. Looking down, Alice caught her breath as a good-sized box turtle made her way inch by inch across the yard.

So after my father died, my sisters and I waited for a sign.

Jennifer's came in the shape of a heart. The hearts started the day she took our mother to the doctors and was told that the cancer was inoperable. When Jennifer got home, there was a small heart made of tissue paper sitting on the front lawn. Not a stain or wrinkle on it. She saw it as a sign from our father and framed it.

Just recently Jen has been visited several times. She has texted each sighting with pictures as proof. "The license plate in front of me says IMHEARTS." We wondered the whys and wherefores of these messages. What are they trying to say? You are not alone. Things will get better. We guess whatever we need to hear.

My signs came to me in the form of electrical energy. Twice it happened while I was vacuuming. Less than a year after my father passed away, I had a 50th birthday party for Tommy Brophy. Upon meeting him twenty-five years earlier, Dad remarked, "When I look at Tommy, I see myself and my brothers when we were young." They too were golden haired boys with carefree attitudes who lost their father when they were young.

The morning after the party, I slept late and then attacked the mess. I opened all the windows and cranked up the music. Placido Domingo's voice vibrated through the room as I collected beer bottles, dumped dips turned to glue and half eaten birthday cake into the garbage. I dragged out the vacuum, plugged it in and started to vacuum while I replayed the night with a sense of satisfaction. My house can handle a crowd and it was packed. Suddenly I stopped and felt a surge as my father's spirit entered my body. I can't explain it any other way. I clearly heard him say, "Great party, Den." And then he was gone.

The second incidence happened while I was living at mother's home in Hampton Bays, the summer after she died. A friend had called and asked for my green bean salad recipe. Since I had rented my house, I didn't have my cookbooks with me.

Later that day while I was vacuuming, I started to cry, missing my mother. Without any particular sign, I put the vacuum down and walked over to a basket crammed with copies of *House Beautiful, Good Housekeeping* and Mom's catalogues. I reached down into the wicker bin and with two fingers pulled out a single sheet of paper with the recipe my friend had asked for.

Besides vacuuming, signs come to me in other electric forms as well. After my mother passed away, my four sisters and I flew to Florida to empty the contents of her home. That night after we were in bed, the light in the laundry room came on and flickered several times. Voices came from bedrooms along the hallway.

"Oh my God."

"Did you see it?"

"What was that?"

My husband Terry and I walked the High Line in New York City this fall. Then we toured the Chelsea Market, which used to be the Nabisco Factory where both his parents had worked before it closed in 1958. Before we left we stopped in the hallway to look at the large black and white photos of the old factory. As Terry was telling me that his mother used to bring home a plain white five-pound box of cookies, one of the ceiling lights went out. We looked up, and it came back on.

❖ ❖ ❖ ❖ ❖

So today when I look down from the bridge to the row of light posts along the road at Shinnecock Park, I'm not surprised that only one lantern is lit. All the others are not. It's daytime. I figure it's a sign from a loved one saying I'm still here watching over you.

The Hunt

August is racing to the finish line. Summer's losing steam. The rosa rugosa flowers that crowd the east side of the bridge have given up and fattened into rose hips, and even a few Queen Ann's Lace have pulled their filigreed skirts around themselves like a cage. I notice two women and a man all dressed in white walking to a boat tied up to the dock. The dark-haired one with a billowing skirt is holding an urn. They are not going fishing.

My parents are buried at Calverton Cemetery. Some people take comfort in visiting their loved ones' graves; I don't. My father got such a kick out of life. When friends greeted him, "How are you George?" He'd respond, "I'm terrific." I try to practice his sense of gratitude and optimism. I also implore his help when I have a golf club in my hand. To visit my mother, I roam around TJMaxx.

My mother loved to shop. Before she learned to drive, she ordered clothes from catalogues that were delivered COD. Sitting with a cup of black coffee on Monday mornings, she would cut out ads from Sunday's papers that decoupaged the dining room table until the following week. Once I asked her about this habit, and she said that after a few days, she really didn't like or need the things she had admired. Kind of window shopping at home. The real shopping began when she got her driver's license. Then she introduced us to bargain stores like Mays or Lanes. Later, we graduated to Loehmann's.

"You can't tell what it looks like on the hanger. You have to try it on." That meant being prodded into the community dressing rooms surrounded by half-naked women. We were modest girls and found it difficult to disrobe while trying not to expose our underwear. While we were in the dressing room, our youngest sister Pam was lying on the floor hiding under a rack of dresses. Inevitably there would be an announcement over the loudspeaker, "Would Pam Gray's mother please report to the customer service desk."

Armed with impeccable taste, a keen eye and indefatigable energy, my mother provided us with beautiful clothing. Later in life when she could have shopped at the finest boutiques, she continued to haunt the stores with the best bargains. It was the love of the hunt, which I have inherited.

My shopping isn't limited to stores. I have discovered estate sales, which in the Hamptons are a quantum leap from yard sales. The prices are often not cheap, but the value is excellent. Besides finding treasures, it's an opportunity to explore tony neighborhoods.

Among my trophy purchases are three large Chinese pots lined in robin's egg blue for one hundred dollars. I paid the same price for the game table in our living room. It's a favorite spot for our grandchildren to play cards, bingo and to work on art projects. When they are older, we'll remove the center panel and teach them to play backgammon on the felt-lined interior. My husband is an Ina Gartner fan, so I was thrilled to find a Kitchen Aid Mix Master like hers for $75 with the bonus of double attachments since it came from a kosher kitchen.

Thanks to my mother, I love fabric. Channeling Scarlett O'Hara, I have turned elegant drapes from estate sales into duvets, shams, dust skirts and slipcovers. Several years ago there was a sale at a large house in town that belonged to a famous upholsterer. The garage and basement were loaded with bolts and bolts of silk, satin, velvet, damask even ones tagged The White House and fine cottons all priced at $2. However, the mold was so bad that you needed a gas mask to spend any length of time in either place. I managed to grab a deep maroon and turquoise paisley. With a little Fabreze and a few days in the sunlight, it smelled like new. The Clarence House material now graces three cushy pillows and a curtain behind the back of our bar.

One of my favorite finds is a six-foot bar with ornate corbels and great storage space. When I walked into the sale in Westhampton, I spied three Waterford goblets like the ones I had inherited from my mother. Then I realized they were lures for me to notice the bar they were sitting on. It took my husband and two nephews to move it, but it is perfect in our family room.

My mother taught me quality, but one hole she left in my education was the art of wrangling. She felt it wasn't ladylike. So haggling does not come naturally to me. My friends joke that I am more inclined to ask, "Is this the most I can pay?" I have progressed to "Can you do better?" I am much more comfortable in an environment where the negotiating has been done for you, and the prices are reduced.

So TJMaxx is a constant in my life, as it was in my mother's. I consider it the binge and purge of shopping because their return policy is so relaxed. Even if I have the receipt and I'm still within the 30-day return policy, I like to get a store credit to keep a revolving account. My step-kids give me TJMaxx gift cards because they know it's the gift that keeps on giving.

When my granddaughter Gabrielle was three I took her to TJMaxx for her first shopping spree. She told me that she would like a pink dress, and a white one, and a brown one too. We fine-combed the racks. Luck was with us; we landed all three. Gabrielle turned eight this year and stills love the hunt. Now our shopping revolves around bagging the perfect Christmas dress. She likes to try on possible purchases in the individual dressing rooms and then model for me. The prize is the moment we look at each other with big smiles and simultaneously agree, "Yes. This is the one."

TJ's was my mother's hunting ground, and I feel her presence there. The year after she died in 2000, I was mindlessly trawling around our favorite store and there on a hook at the end of an aisle was my wedding dress, a long white fitted chiffon gown with subtle beading for $95. Thank you, Mom. Even on the rare occasions when I don't find something, I am happy to be there sighting labels, rubbing fabric between my fingers, checking for generous hems and matching seams.

❖❖❖❖❖

Before I head towards my car at Ponquogue Beach, I watch the boat, with the three passengers and their precious cargo, trailing a silver wake make its way to the inlet and out into the sea. The opening words of my mother's eulogy echo through my head:

"TJMaxx has lost a loyal customer; the UPS man has one less stop; a catalogue company or two will probably fold, and my sisters and I have lost our mother."

Atlantis

On the way to the bridge I pass a gingerbread house that sits on Foster Avenue like a story book character. Pumpkins have sprouted on the front porch and corn stalks guard the front door. On the edge of the property a garage is still painted like a red, white and blue stripped flag. Next door is The Beach Bar, now Shuckers, which was built after the Oliver Twist Inn burned down.

The Oliver Twist Inn was a favorite summer bar in the 60s. I remember one night in particular. The large patio that wrapped around the front of the building was packed. The group who rented the neighboring house was having a party where a guy with a megaphone was drawing a crowd with the familiar words, "Faster than a speeding bullet, more powerful than a locomotive, able to leap tall buildings with a single bound...it's Superman." With that, a young man appeared on the roof of the garage in full costume. He struck an imposing posture, flung open his cape and flew into the crowd. Friends below were prepared to catch him. Another masked marvel followed to the cheers of the crowd.

That memory reminded me of a costume party I hosted in the late 1980s before the wave of friends' fortieth birthday parties. Although it didn't require daring feats like jumping off a building, it did call for shedding traditional roles and stepping out of comfort zones. The invitation that I pieced together from newspaper clippings, like a ransom note, dared my friends to come dressed as famous performers ready to lip sync their songs.

Thirty years later they still talk about that party. When I ask my friends why that night was so memorable, their first response is how drunk we were, which is true because most of us were nervous about being center stage, so we did imbibe more than usual. It wasn't like other parties where you just show up with flowers or a bottle of wine. This involved the pressure of first deciding on a role, then trying to capture the look of that person, choosing a song and practicing your act. This personal investment as well as anticipation fueled our fear or excitement.

Tommy Brophy and Pat Maas, two funny guys, outdid the Blues Brothers. Even their body types matched Dan Aykroyd and John Belushi. In black suits and hats and dark glasses they perfectly imitated the hop steps and hand motions of Elwood and Jakes' 1980 Saturday Night Live skit. We all collapsed in laughter as they belted out "Soul Man."

Jill and Dave Kandell were a new couple then. Dave, a widower with a young son, was courting Jill, a rising star in the real estate world. As Kiki Dee and Elton John they sang "Don't Go Breaking My Heart." A year later we were at their wedding on Dune Road. I met them recently when they were enjoying "the best view around" on the Ponquogue Bridge. We joked that they hadn't broken each other's hearts.

An early follower of Billy Joel, Richie Bach in jeans and a muscle shirt danced around his adoring wife Terry as he sang "Uptown Girl." In his element, he acted as Master of Ceremonies and stage hand when technical assistance was needed. Over the years Richie, an orthodontist, pursued his avocation and became a song writer with frequent trips to Nashville.

One of my favorite performers was Frank Marotta, Tony Bennett incarnate. Suave in a tuxedo, microphone in hand, he crooned "I left My Heart in San Francisco" as he worked the audience, choosing sexy harlette, Kathy Bodkin to serenade. I don't think Frank's wife, Liz, even noticed. She was paralyzed with dread and so uncomfortable with performing that it actually helped her Janis Joplin rant. Who could forget Jack Helm as Al Jolson and Gabe Ariola's Rastafarian look and accessories?

Other acts included Diane and Max Salvatore, ever the debonair couple, dressed in black with top hats and canes as they soft shoed to " Me and My Shadow." Covered in purple balloons, Joanna and Vic Levy entertained us with "Heard It Through the Grapevine." The white Supremes--Jeanne Brophy, Debbie Maas and Susan Claudio--with matching bouffant hairdos, evening gowns, and elbow length gloves raised their right hands and sang "Stop in the Name of Love."

I couldn't spare the time to practice with a group, so I decided to be Cyndi Lauper and spent my 45 minute commute memorizing the words to "Girls Just Want to Have Fun" while trying to envision an outrageous outfit. I settled on a black tank top, green tutu, fishnet stockings and high tops. I spiked my short hair and applied cherry lipstick and sapphire blue eye shadow.

But the girls who had the most fun were the ones who dressed as The Shangri-Las. The suburban moms easily morphed into tough gum-smacking sluts. My slim thirty-something friends found the shortest black latex dresses, which they enhanced with more than generous padding. Heavy eyeliner, red lips and big hair completed the look. The high light was their skit of "Leader of the Pack." Despite the minibike Paul Levandowski rode, he maintained authority in his leather as the Leader of the Pack.

Sue, Ann, Eileen, Joanne and Kathy, my con-servative friends, entered the makeshift stage in black graduation robes dressed as nuns singing "How Do You Solve a Problem like Marie?" Mid-song they slipped out of the robes into their roles as the Harlettes.

Costumes can be so liberating.

Since the Harlettes' routine was complicated, the girls needed to rehearse. So while I was at work, they set up in the living room on the second floor of my house to practice. Or was it to perform for the guys who had a bird's eye view while they were working on my neighbor's roof?

Speaking of voyeurism, Doug Penny, former Southampton Town Supervisor, was the only one who didn't come in a costume. He claimed his job was to film our production. There were so many videos of the party, I think even Hampton Bays Library had one.

At the end of the night we formed a semi-circle, arms linked around each other, and swayed to our rendition of "We Are the World."

❖ ❖ ❖ ❖ ❖

Like the back of a beached whale, the large sandbar east of the Ponquogue Bridge has risen. Since it is under water half of the time, there is no vegetation, so the birds don't claim it. Stinky Island, Party Isle, Lovette Landing, it has as many names as the groups who party there.

My party gave rise to a different side of us that disappeared the next day. But we know our alternate personalities lie just below the surface.

Riptide

I join a few early walkers on the Ponquogue Bridge as the sun cracks open the horizon. When I reach the ocean pavilion it's empty, but there are two abandoned coffee cups side by side on one of the picnic tables. I wonder how many affairs begin with the invitation, "Just have coffee with me." Actually ours started with champagne; the coffee came later.

He and his wife had been on the outer circle of my social life. He and I always sought each other out at parties, and there were a lot of parties. Tall and dark, I can picture him dressed as Abe Lincoln at a Halloween bash. His energy lit up a room. A great listener, he focused on me like a laser.

That night he and his wife along with a large group of friends attended a Hospice Benefit under a tent in Westhampton. I was wearing a glamorous creation purchased at a consignment shop: short, sleeveless, cream knit sheath with ten inches of organza tulle at the hem--not my usual Hampton casual look. Champagne corks popped before the party officially began.

Towards the end of the night I sensed him behind me. I turned and looked up. Words I couldn't take back bubbled out, "Remember when you asked me if I ever lose control? If I did, I'd be all over you."

He grabbed my wrist. "I've been in love with you for years."

"No.No.No."

He folded me into his arms, and we began to dance. At that moment I knew nothing would ever be the same. Like pulling the wrong cube from a Jenga tower, my married life had just collapsed.

Overcome by a sense of panic, the next day I swore off drinking until the next time I would swear off drinking. I called a friend for the name of her therapist, went to church, something I only do for weddings and funerals, trying to create a dam for the surge I felt coming.

After a week went by with no sightings of him, no phone calls, hang ups, or wrong numbers, I relaxed a little. But the following Monday he was parked next to my car when I came out of work. He opened the door, walked around his jeep and stood smiling sheepishly at me. His expression was often like someone ready to tell a joke.

Forty-five minutes from home. "Did you just happen to be in the neighborhood?"

"I wanted to see you. To talk."

"I don't think it's a good idea."

He moved closer and gazed at me with his intense eyes, "Just have coffee with me." He took my hand and led me to my car.

We slid into a green booth at Friendly's and made a pretense of looking at the menu.

"We can't do this." I told him that it would be disastrous and would never happen. "It's not fair to our spouses. Suppose they find out?"

I don't remember what he said. Maybe he just listened, then confessed his feelings for me. "I know you feel the same."

Deny, deny, deny. Shaking my head, "It was the champagne; it's wrong."

"Take my cell number." He wrote it down on the back of his placemat and handed it to me. I ripped it up when I got into my car, but by the end of the week I had pieced the papers together and called him.

We met at the ocean pavilion where we huddled with our backs against the south facing wall sheltered from the wind. Two cars drove into the parking lot. What were we thinking? Are we out of our minds? Even in the off season someone will see us.

Thus began a series of meetings on back roads, deserted sites, and secrets places.

What I didn't know then was I was trying to suck his passion for life into mine. What I didn't know then was his guilt would make sex frustrating. What I didn't know then was this wasn't his first affair, but he would tell his wife about me and that he was leaving. What I didn't know then was he wouldn't.

What I knew was he was all that mattered. With him I felt unzipped, split open, delivered. I had opened myself, exposed a vulnerability that I hadn't surrendered to my husband. I was ready to walk out of my marriage so fast it shocked me.

That first year I actually believed that we would live happily ever after. In my head I decorated the bedrooms vacated by my college age children and deposited his children in my fairyland. Ironically, part of his appeal was his role as a family man, which a divorce would have destroyed.

After a year, worn down by emotion, reason started to surface. I told my husband, Jack, I was unhappy and needed a little time by myself .I stayed at a girlfriend's house to compose myself. Jack had told me several times in our marriage that if I was ever unfaithful to him, our marriage would be over. It would have been easier to tell him I wanted a divorce than to confess that I was having an affair.

One of the things that impressed me during the short time I stayed with my friend was her stocked pantry. It was stuffed with boxes of pasta, cereal, cake mixes, cookies, crammed with cans of tomatoes, soup, beans, tins of tuna fish and rows of bottles of oils, vinegar and juices--all for one person. I pictured my shelves where you could count the items with empty spaces between them. An obedient wife, I had tried to stay within a husband-dictated household budget.

Returning to a starving marriage, I asked my husband to go to counseling with me. Can this twenty plus-year marriage be saved? Our roles were so deeply entrenched. After a few sessions my husband felt sabotaged because he thought the therapist's purpose was to validate my issues. He was probably right. He stopped therapy; I continued.

My therapist had said, "Your boyfriend is Russian roulette for you." At that point I told my lover that we needed to stop seeing each other.

But I knew he would be back. A month later he was standing at my back door with coffee just the way I like it. I had no guilt. Lies slipped off my tongue.

He told me that as long as I stayed married I would be his. And it was true. The affair was no longer a romantic movie but a painful reality. I had gotten a glimpse of what I was missing, but it was like opening a present that wasn't mine. I fought the rip current the affair had thrown me into, but I couldn't free myself for two years.

When I looked in the mirror, I expected to see some woman with a scarlet letter embroidered on her chest but it was just me, except it wasn't. By the third year I understood that when I left my marriage, I would be alone. Although I had felt a void in my heart for years, the word divorce was not in my vocabulary. I didn't want to enter that alien life, but I couldn't live with the stranger I had become. I had ridden the current. Now it was time to swim parallel with the shore and surf a wave in.

In the final days this man, who I had wrapped my life around, was a wreck. He walked a tension wire between his wife, who knew about us, and me. Running his fingers through his long hair he cried, "I can't be happy with you. I can't be happy with her. I am falling apart."

"Why don't you see my shrink? He knows all about you anyway." And he did. My therapist had said that people have affairs to stay in a marriage or to leave it. I couldn't stay; he couldn't leave.

❖❖❖❖❖

I sit for a while on the deck of the Ponquogue Pavilion scanning the surf for the rip tide that has menaced swimmers this summer .While I am looking for churned surfaces that differ in color from surrounding water, I hear a dripping sound. The faucet that bathers use to wash their feet is stuck in the on position. I try, but I can't turn it off.

Confession

On the bridge, I see what looks like long thin clouds or maybe a sky writer because they form a perfect x. X marks the spot. This is the place to be. A woman talking on a cell phone passes me and I catch a snippet of her conversation: "I want to say I am sorry."

Instantly I flash back to the day I apologized to the wife of my former lover. That day she and I crossed paths three times. We were on the same line at the Post Office. I could tell by the set of her jaw that she knew I was behind her. When she left, we didn't make eye contact. An hour later I was sitting at the nail salon in one of the pedicure thrones when she walked in, spotted me and walked out. Finally, at lunch time we both ended up at the same deli. His wife was leaving as I walked in. Our eyes met and I started, "I think we were meant to meet today. I'd like to talk to you if you have a minute."

The last time we spoke was three years ago. She called me. I immediately recognized her voice. Her husband had told her that he was leaving her for me. She was calm, non-threatening. If I had been in her position, I would have been raging and violent. We met on a deserted country road. She was there when I pulled up. I parked, walked over to her car. She opened the door and I got in.

"Thanks for coming."

I didn't know what to say, so I waited.

"I have always liked you. I know you are a nice person and I am begging you for time." She told me that she couldn't believe that he would give up his family and all they had worked for. She asked me to not see him for a short time so she could have a chance to work things out. If they couldn't, she wouldn't stand in my way. We sat breathing the same air in semi-darkness, outside it was raining leaves. I nodded and started to cry. And then we were both sobbing in each other's arms. Loving the same man is a strange bond.

Now it was my turn to talk. We left the deli and we walked outside, "I want you to know that I am truly sorry I have caused you so much pain."

Her face slackened and her eyes welled up. I continued nervously. "He made his decision. He loves you. He chose you."

She wasn't responding, but she was listening. I added, "I admire you for fighting to keep your man. You must love him very much. I pushed on. "I think you are kind of lucky in a way. Your issues are out on the table. You have a chance to make things better. Divorce is my option."

I paused, "I want to reassure you that I won't be with him again." I looked deeply into her eyes to seal the promise.

We turned and headed in separate directions to our cars.

❖❖❖❖❖

At home, I note that the last of the orange day lilies that have greeted me each morning are gone. Their brown stalks, summer skeletons, need to be pulled, but it's been so hot. Yesterday's heat and humidity are gone today.

Tartan Plaid Pajamas

No bridge today. It's raining. I decide to do something I rarely do, stay in my pajamas all day. Since I have no place I have to be, I am content rotating between the couch and the red and white checked swivel chair at my writing desk. Except for Thanksgiving, November doesn't have much to offer. It's like a conjunction connecting the autumnal display of October and the joyous season of December. Plus my father died in November.

We buried Dad a half a dozen times. Between his weak heart and bouts of cancer we anticipated his funeral with every reoccurrence. My mother, who had a master's degree in denial, called at 8:30 on a Saturday morning. She was having a hard time with our ailing father. She wanted one of us to come down to Florida and help bring him home. I panicked. I don't know what was more shocking, my mother calling at that hour or her asking for help.

I hung up the phone and repeated the conversation to my son. He grounded me. "Mom, if Grandma said sometime soon, you better leave today."

In my previous life as eldest of five, I would have stoically handled every detail assuring my sisters not to worry. But my upper lip had lost its starch that decade. In the end, my sister Suzan and I left for Florida. My mother was vague, but we felt she thought our father was dying.

On the flight down I envisioned the wake. The flower-filled double room was crowded. I am standing with my daughter and son near a table with a water carafe and a box of Kleenex. Across the laughter and conversations that rise and fall, I see my former lover standing in the doorway. Our eyes lock; we move toward each other. He envelops me, and I finally break down. One arm holds me tightly against his chest and the other cradles my head where he rests his face kissing my hair. It doesn't matter to either of us that my children and former husband stare at us and wonder why his wife isn't with him and when he and I had become so close. For the moment he is there for me. The man who has always loved me has died. I need to be comforted by a former love because there is no current love.

At my parents' home in Florida, my father's friends filtered in and out saying their "final" good-byes. I don't think my father felt the same way. In a sense it seemed like we were kidnapping him. He seemed too weak to object or maybe he thought it was best for our mother.

Back in Hampton Bays for six raw November days, my father dressed in unmatched pajamas covered by an afghan sat in his chair in front of the TV. On the seventh day, I was there when George P. Gray was resurrected. He appeared in black slacks, a crisp white shirt topped with a black argyle cashmere sweater, his hair slicked back with Vitalis. He announced, "Damn it Betty, I'm not dying. We are going back to Florida."

I clung to him. "Daddy, I am so afraid I will never see you again."

"Now, now Den. I'll be home before you know it."

A year later he came home in a coffin. My mother and the five of us were blessed to be with him when the death rattle stopped and we inhaled his final exhale.

Before we flew back to New York, my sisters and I took a piece or two of our father's clothing. That night I slept alone in his green tartan plaid pajamas.

Span 15

Covered Bridges

The skyscape this morning looks like a postcard from Lake Tahoe. Mountainous clouds and a conifer forest covered in snow rim a circle of dazzling cobalt blue. Lake Tahoe was the destination of my first vacation as a divorced woman in the early 90's.

I got a call from my friend Susan. "Hey Denise. Any chance you'd wanna go to Lake Tahoe for the February break? My roommate just backed out."

"I don't have any plans yet. That might be great. Do you think I could cross country ski?"

"I don't see why not. There's tons of snow."

It seemed like a great idea to get away after the divorce. During my married years before our children were in college, we spent winter break at our house in Vermont. I was looking forward to cross country skiing again.

After we arrived at the Reno-Tahoe Airport we shared a van with ten people, like a circus act with skis and baggage. I had the feeling it wasn't going to be the kind of vacation I had become accustomed to. If I had done a little research I would have known that the lake straddles two states. Its northern shores are in peaceful tree-hugging California, while the southern side in Nevada welcomes the gambling party crowd.

I longed to be up in those lofty peaks with a view of the alpine lake that is so deep it never freezes. Instead much of my vacation was spent in downtown tawdry Tahoe. We stayed at Harvey's Hotel and Gambling Casino. It's on Tahoe's main strip across the street from another casino, down the block from six more. Actually, Harvey's and Harrah's Casinos are connected by an underground tunnel.

I don't like to gamble. I don't know which I hate more, losing money or being inside smoked-filled windowless rooms with people who spend their days feeding coins into a machine. Since I had planned to be outside most of the time anyway, I could live with the fact that this place lacked the charm of a country inn or the rustic welcome of a family lodge.

The next morning I pushed the drapes aside and looked out the window at a wall of white. The skies had opened during the night and dumped snow that would fall steadily for days. Everything came to a standstill. Few vehicles challenged the blizzard conditions. The slopes would remain closed for a third of our holiday. Marooned at Harvey's.

After breakfast Susan and I decided to explore the hotel. To my dismay there were no quiet public areas at Harvey's. Nowhere you could nestle into a couch, sit in front of a fire and spend an afternoon absorbed in a good read. We ventured through the tunnel to check out Harrah's and found more of the same. The smell of cigarette smoke, the ding, ding, dinging, and coin clicking of slot machines were pervasive.

Back at Harvey's, Susan, who is single and ten years younger than I, decided to see if any of her downhill ski friends were at the bar.

"Have fun. I have some reading to catch up on. I'll see you at dinner." At fifty and recently divorced, the idea of drinking the afternoon away with strangers had no appeal. Two days passed.

On the third day the snow took a break, and we were rescued by close friends staying outside of town. Our families had vacationed together in Vermont. I couldn't help feeling that if I was still married, I too would be snug in a cozy condo up on the mountain instead of down on the main drag. They had a four-wheel-drive Land Rover and chauffeured us between the movies and their place where we played board games and worked on completing a 1,000 piece puzzle.

Those old-fashioned indoor activities reminded me of the happy times with my children at our Vermont chalet at Bolton Valley Ski Resort. Once you made it up that mountain road and negotiated the steep driveway, you stayed. It was a ski-in, ski-out type of place, where the kids were safe on their own during the day. By 4:00 everyone would be home either on the deck peeling off outer garments, soaking up the afternoon sun, sipping hot chocolate or in the living room lounging on the couches in front of a roaring fire. A pot of sauce with meatballs and sausage, or a hearty stew, or soup would be simmering on the stove. I loved being in that family bubble surrounded by natural beauty. Here at Tahoe we listened to the boom- boom of dynamiting to control the threat of avalanches.

When the lifts were open on the fourth day, I was on my own since my roommate, our friends and the fellow travelers in the van were all downhillers. Dressed in layers with my skis over my shoulder, I approached the man at the front desk to ask about cross country skiing trails and was told there weren't any nearby. However, I could take the public bus on the corner and then transfer to another bus to a park ten miles away. A 30 minute to an hour commute depending on traffic, connections, weather etc. I couldn't believe it. Too complicated. Too much effort.

I slumped back to my room and into bed. It didn't take much to push me deeper into the drift I was in. By then the voices in my head were raging, *What the hell are you doing here? Maybe my mother was right. Is this what being divorced means? Feeling like a second-class citizen? Is this my future? Get used to it.* The walls of the room closed in on me. My innerscape was in a white out.

Although my spirits were in a slump, my appetite wasn't. At midday I dragged myself out of bed and walked down the block. The New York Café called to me. I ordered a burger and then hung out drinking coffee, playing solitaire and writing the same thing in my journal over and over again like a punishment for misbehaving in class. "I hate this place. I am surrounded by nature's playground, but I can't get to it. I am on the inside looking out. I hate this place."

On the way back to Harvey's, I stopped on the sidewalk where a plaque had been cleared of snow. There you could stand in two states at the same time. Placing one foot in California, the other in Nevada, I touched the groove on my ring finger left by the wedding band I had worn for twenty-five years. Part of me still felt married. It was like I was wearing my shoes on the wrong feet.

Back at the New York Café the next day, I continued my journaling. "I hate this place" scribble splintered off into what I had expected from the divorce: freedom and independence. I underplayed the loss of a comfortable lifestyle and the reality of being without a mate. I couldn't have appreciated those factors until I experienced them. Before that they were just words. The truth was I was frightened by this new life I had chosen. Without the comfort of my children, my home and a man at my side, I was freefalling. I had to grope across this bridge between one life and another

These feelings made me think of the covered bridges in Vermont, those quaint structures that from a distance look like a barn suspended in midair. I make a point to drive or walk across one when I'm in the Green Mountain State.

Moving through the darkness into the light is like traveling through a poem. Massive timber trusses support the roofs that shelter travelers from the snow. Some people say that the purpose was to hide the view of the water below from the horses, so they wouldn't be spooked while crossing..

Experience had taught me that being in nature is how I renew and recharge. It would be a waste to fly across the country and spend my last days inside feeling sorry for myself. With only two days left I decided to get the bus schedules, find the park, and do what I had come here for. I needed to go cross country skiing, to ingest the awesomeness and serenity outside myself, and to be reminded I am a speck in the universe.

On the first bus, my skis and poles standing tall, I sat next to silent local people like props going to work or doctor appointments. They probably would not have been a sympathetic audience for my complaints, "I am having the worst vacation. It really sucks that with all this snow there isn't someplace closer where I can ski."

At the end of the line, I got off, waited ten minutes and then boarded another local bus. I double-checked with the driver that I was where I was supposed to be. Twenty minutes later he called out, "Lady, this is your stop. Take a left at the corner. The park's two blocks down." I checked in with the attendant and was told that I was the only one on the trails. They closed in two hours.

Changing into my Nordic shoes, I clicked into the skis and glided onto the flat trail. For the first time on this trip I felt normal. It dawned on me that skiing was always a solitary experience for me since my family and friends were downhill skiers. During the first hour I slapped the skis down and pushed off from side to side building speed until I was sweating, and I stripped down to my long underwear, jacket tied around my waist.

Deeper into the woods, I slowed down. I listened to the whisper of the softly falling snow, the creak of an old branch, my breath puffing into empty balloon captions. I stopped. The tips of my skis sat like periscopes breaking the surface of the snow. Majestic fir trees draped in ermine and dangling crystals embraced me, and I fell into the grace of this other world. I breathed it in and moved on.

Giant Steps

The sky surrounding the bay hangs like a long grey skirt with a darker hem lifted to show the tiniest bit of white. With the humidity at 97 percent, I want to get in a walk before the skies burst open. I look up and notice that the top of the tower at the Coast Guard Station has disappeared like Jack's beanstalk into the clouds.

I felt like Jill climbing the bean stalk when in 1994 Jim Mahoney, my mentor, suggested that I apply for a National Endowment for the Humanities Summer Seminar. Jim, chairman of our English Department, was an innovative leader; I was his disciple. Newly divorced and on my own for the first time in twenty-five years, it was an intellectual and personal giant step he felt I was ready to take. I wasn't so sure.

There were sixty-nine seminars offered across the United States. Stipends were awarded according to the length of the seminar four, five and six weeks. The programs provided teachers with the opportunity to work under the supervision of a distinguished professor and active scholar in various fields. Applicants were required to submit an essay along with letters of recommendation.

After perusing the NEH catalogue, I narrowed my choices to First Novels of American Indians at Bellingham University in Washington and Twentieth Century Segregated South through Autobiography at the University of North Carolina at Wilmington. I chose the latter because I knew I could write a convincing essay.

I was a fan of Maya Angelou. Her autobiography *I Know Why the Caged Bird Sings* was one of the required readings. Scrawled on the top of my journal are her words "Most people want exchange not change." I incorporated lines from her poem, *On the Pulse of the Morning,* read at Clinton's inauguration, in my application.

The letters colleagues penned on my behalf made me feel that winning the fellowship would be a bonus. I carefully sealed my paperwork with an Elvis stamp, anxious to make an impression any way I could. I was wait-listed the first year and accepted the following summer.

On the last day of school I arrived in Big Red, the clunky Chevy station wagon a friend of my mother's had bequeathed to me. My sexy Saab had died. Free is a tough price to resist; humility is a virtue. The car was jammed with everything I could possibly need for the next month or two including a three liter tin of olive oil. My house was rented for the summer. Everything in closets and cupboards had to be cleaned, stored, thrown out or packed in my car.

My friends stood by the curb in the parking lot at school waving good-bye. Alice, our librarian, reminded me I was welcome to use her condo in Caroline Beach if I met a cute guy. I imagined tin cans tied to the bumper of my car below a sign that read "Just Single." I rapped out the words from my poem *Solo*.

> I am Bonnie sans Clyde
> Thelma without Louise
> Gonna do whatever I please.
> Traveling solo for the first time
> Wished I'd done it in my prime.
> Batteries are charged
> Hoping to get my life enlarged.
> Papers have been signed
> Leaving it all behind.
> Destination — peace of mind.

When I reached Richmond, Virginia, I pulled into the Holiday Inn where I had a reservation. In my room I found a man's suit hanging in the closet. Wow, I thought, they really do have more amenities than I expected. I toyed with a romantic movie version but went back to the front desk where I was told they only had a single size room available. Practically in tears I cried, "I've been in my car for twelve hours. I need a room bigger than a box."

The manager, who happened to be at the desk, rescued me. "I think the suite might be available." It wasn't luxurious, but it was cavernous. I called room service and ordered a bottle of merlot and a rib eye steak. I ended the day soaking in a tub big enough for a party. As I sunk into the bubbles I thought, "This is a good omen."

There were 15 of us from all over the United States and two foreign students. Unlike me, a middle school Language Arts teacher, most taught high school history and some were published writers. I felt like I was in the wrong classroom.

The syllabus included four required autobiographies equally divided by race and sex, as well as two other texts, additional reading and a final paper. Guest lectures, films and road trips rounded out a full program.

We lived in barrack like dorms on the flat campus. Despite a heavy work load we squeezed in some good times. Meals were the highlight of our days. A pig pickin' at our professor's house was our first communal meal. The thing I remember most was that fact that no alcohol was served. That was not an issue at a shrimp boil on the beach or our last supper at a microbrewery in Wilmington. In between there were times to sit on the cool cement steps in the shade drinking beer and talking.

Coming from a lily-white world, I learned more about race relations outside the classroom than from any of the books we read. One of my colleagues, Big John, a serious black man, was threatened when he went for a walk through an area neighboring the college. He told me that there was the paper bag test at Morehouse College when he was a student. To be accepted into the most popular fraternity, candidates had to have skin as light as a brown paper bag.

One of my classmates, originally from the area, invited us to his mother's Southern Baptist church. "I have to warn you that the service is three hours long, but the food afterwards will be worth it."

My first question, "What should I wear?"

"Something like what you would wear to church. A dress or a skirt."

Afraid of being underdressed and disrespectful, I asked, "How about a hat?"

He shook his head, "Oh no. Only the older ladies wear them."

The congregation was composed of mainly women in hats. In between the foot-stomping, hand-clapping, music of a washboard, tambourine and spoons, the minister asked if anyone had something they wanted to share. Then the real entertainment began. Midway through the testimonials I saw the light and felt compelled to stand up and give thanks. Folks responded, "Praise the Lord." The last woman to speak ended with "alleluias", which she repeated like soft foreplay escalating into a loud explosive climax. The minister simply prayed, "Better out than in sister."

An African American woman from Louisiana, the youngest in our group, challenged us to go to a black social club one night, insisting that we should see how it felt to be in the minority. After we passed through a metal detector at the front door, the owner greeted us, "Y'all must be from out of town." He went out of his way to make us feel welcome. The male patrons enjoyed the novelty and asked us to dance, but the women kept their distance. We didn't stay long. When we told Doctor McLaurin, our professor, about the experience he laughed, "You were in deep cotton."

I blurted out, "Does that mean deep shit?"

"No, Denise, that was the place for the well-to-do blacks."

Just recently while listening to NPR, Michelle Norris was interviewing a Professor McLaurin, author of *The Marines of Montford Point: American's First Black Marines*. It caught my attention because I recognized the name and the voice. When she addressed him as Melton, I realized that she was speaking to the man who had run my seminar close to twenty years ago.

My gay hairdresser from home was vacationing in Wilmington and invited me to a party. I didn't know what to expect. The Village People of YMCA fame played like video in my head. But the family gala in a penthouse atop the tallest building in town was an elegant affair that exuded southern charm and hospitality. Crystal champagne flutes stood in formation on a sideboard groaning with flakey biscuits, country ham, fried chicken, North Carolina vinegary barbeque, and collard greens cooked with bacon.

During a field trip to Charleston with Professor McLauren, I was also able to spend an overnight with old friends, Jimmy and Janet Rowe. They lived outside of Charleston across the Ashley River on Sulllvan Island, where we had enjoyed many holidays and school vacations. Jimmy grew up with my former husband in Maryland.

After dinner we sat on their screened-in porch where citronella candles cast shadows of a ladder back chair against the front wall of the house. We talked about the divorce, which I had initiated. As a southeast wind teased distant chimes, my former best man gave me final absolution, "I am surprised you didn't do it sooner." Dark clouds cleared on that sweltering South Carolina night unveiling the moon full and ripe.

Along with immersing myself in southern autobiography, dispelling myths and stereotypes, I experimented with relationships down south as well. At age 49, a virgin branded to one man for most of my life, I needed a refresher course in Men 101. I was attracted to Joe in our group. He grew up on Long Island and was a published poet living in Connecticut. One night he shared "Great Neck Girls," "Catholic Girl" and "Southampton Summer," which he had written before he met me. I was a Catholic girl who grew up in Great Neck and lived in the town just west of Southampton. I fell in love with his poetry.

We stayed in touch for several years after the program taking the Port Jefferson Ferry back and forth to spend the weekend together. To me it was part of the romance. Joe, sometimes with flowers, would be there waiting on the dock looking like a well-groomed hippie. White hair and mustache, a modern Mark Twain, his jeans and tweed jacket hung on his athletic body. I tried to fall in love with him, but his negative energy was familiar and exhausting.

While we were on campus, the women in my group discouraged my attention to Joe and directed me to focus on Will, a tall pleasant guy from California. My friend Alice had offered me use of her Carolina Beach Condo. At the end of the seminar, I called her giggling "Send the key."

Will and I spent a week there. With him I felt safe to let go and be. Life was simple: bed, bread and beach. We spooned on the sand, two middle-aged lovers under a Dutch Boy blue sky. I named it the imperfect beach for all the women with the fleshy folds in their belly-busting bikinis. I called him jungle boy. He had a swimmer's golden body with tight curls gelled around the nape of his neck. Only I pictured them longer and loose, a wild nest of ringlets. He called me a hoody nice girl because I guzzled beer from the bottle, had a taste for expletives and an appetite for sex.

I visited him once in California. When I left, we wished the best for each other. I shared with him my fears of serial monogamy. Kissing a lot of frogs made me a frogette. The last time I talked to him, he was with a woman he thought he loved, and I still hadn't found my prince.

Being on a college campus as a middle-aged woman also reinforced the fact that I was no longer a cute co-ed. But I felt like I had gotten my groove back. At the beach one day I had on a marine blue halter top bathing suit with a batik sarong tied around my hips. My hair was wet. Standing at the bar waiting for a beer I heard a young guy drawl to his girlfriend, "I bet she was something twenty years ago." She responded, "I think she looks pretty good now."

By the end of the summer, I had taken the seminar into the palm of my hands and molded it into the shape of my most private needs. That time at University of North Carolina made me appreciate that giant steps are generally followed by many baby steps, putting one foot in front of the other.

A Super Woman

While I look from my vantage point atop the Ponquogue Bridge, an easterly wind splashes the bay onto the splintered embankment creating water fountains. Serious cyclists fly past me followed by Sunday riders straining with each downward stroke, and beginners pedaling madly because they haven't clicked into the right gear.

For a summer or two my former husband, a disciplined athlete with overdeveloped calves, got into biking, and I tagged along. He organized outings that increased in mileage and difficulty for a small group of friends, most of whom would have been content with a mile or two to the nearest deli.

After a harrowing ride from Hampton Bays to Sag Harbor on two lane roads with no shoulders and traffic so close you could feel the swish of speeding cars, we all dropped out of the group. My ex started to ride with the cyclists at Rotations Bicycle Center in Southampton. We were moving in different directions.

Several years later after I got divorced, my cousin Hedy, who lived and biked in Colorado, came to visit. During her stay two world class cyclists, a tall man and a petite woman were scheduled to give a talk at Rotations followed by a ride through the north side of Southampton. I thought Hedy would really enjoy it. Since I had some biking background, including a weekend with the Vermont Bicycle Tours, I would go too. I failed to remember that being a flatlander, I had walked the bike almost as much as I rode it on those mountain roads.

I spent a good deal of the lecture checking out our fellow bikers. Everyone seemed to be dressed in Lycra with the latest accessories. When I saw all the titanium bikes lined up outside next to my ten speed, I realized I was out of my league. But how bad could it be? Long Island is flat except for the circuit we were on, which I swear rivaled the trails of the Green Mountain State.

The twenty-mile ride was tortuous. The pack immediately broke away, so there was no chance of drafting. After the first mile I couldn't even see the other riders, they were so far ahead of me. I was alone. Beads of perspiration slid down my face and cupped in my ears. Rivulets ran down my sides. Drenched in sweat from nerves and exertion, I alternated between grinding gears and spinning wheels.

At each rest station I was the last to arrive. Actually, I wonder if there were supposed to be any stops. Hedy sailed ahead with the other cyclists. By the last leg, a sheer incline, I had hit the wall. I was standing on my pedals willing them to move when the female professional rider whipped down the hill, came up behind me, placed her hand on the small of my back and pushed me up the hill like a super woman.

That bike ride became symbolic for all the times someone has given me the push I needed, taught me to switch gears, and helped me when I couldn't do it alone. I thought being divorced would be easier than it was. I needed help negotiating this unfamiliar terrain during those six years before I met my husband Terry.

My therapist had warned me not to expect much from the dating scene. I would be lucky if I had a date or two a year. Anticipating the busy social life I had in college, I thought, uh, maybe other women, not me. I didn't appreciate how dry the well is at mid-century. Besides trying to find love, I had to learn to be okay by myself. It took me a while before I realized I had those two things in the wrong order.

I had never lived on my own; I had gone from college to marriage. Simple things like eating alone, going to the movies without a date, coming home to a dark empty house took some getting used to. I found Oprah to be an engaging dinner partner; I sat in the aisle seat at matinees, and I adopted a cat.

Hedy, who was also divorced, became my guiding star. I lived with her in Colorado during the summer of '96. Between hiking, river rafting and road trips, she modeled how to live as a single woman. Together we read and discussed books as we traveled a spiritual path where I could develop powers of my own. Those emotional and mental muscles didn't develop overnight, but I knew that although I was lonely, I wasn't alone.

She suggested that I give my *House Beautiful* and *More* magazines a break and broaden the scope of my reading material. *Men's Journal* gave me insight into the male psyche and the best recipe for braised pork shoulder. I had vicarious adventures perusing articles in *Patagonia* catalogues and the *NY Times* Travel pages. In addition to the Style section, I added the Business and Metropolitan news to my weekly reading.

Hedy had a library of the *Idiots Guide to Home Maintenance and Repair* and radiated a roll-up-your-sleeves can-do attitude. And if you can't, hire a cute guy.

Because of her I joined Habitat for Humanity, and when they asked me to do the coffee run, I said, "Sure. First give me a hammer. I want to bang some nails." My name is set in the cement walls in the basement of the first Habitat house in our area located on Sagg Pike.

Then there was the dating scene/booty calls. My friends thought I had gone off my rocker. I had become a middle-aged slut. Why would I even talk to that guy again? Hedy understood.

But the main thing my cousin did for me was to tell me over and over again that I would be fine and that everything would be okay. It was hard to accept that message from well-meaning married friends, but because Hedy had been riding solo for a few years and knew me well, I believed her.

❖❖❖❖❖

Coming home from the beach today, I scanned the macadam surface below the bridge for the T bar that looks like a scarecrow with free, loaner, yellow life vests hanging from it. Sponsored by Sea Tow and Clare Rose following several boating accidents, the idea was to encourage the use of floatation devices. I thought of Hedy and other friends who kept me afloat when I was in water over my head.

Gazing up the walkway, the sun casts a shadow of my arm three times its normal size. I laugh. I look like a super woman. Who could I push up the hill?

Naked

Long breakers trundle in from the sea with spray foam crests. The front rows of the parking lot at Ponquogue Beach are filled. There are four-wheel drives with racks on top and neatly stacked surf boards. Topless Jeeps are parked with the sharklike fins of their boards sticking out the rear. And there are the work trucks driven by guys trying to squeeze in a few waves during lunch break. The surfers are in various stages of undress: bare backs, biceps, chests, and legs. An array of public nakedness.

Growing up in a family of five girls, we were very modest. I remember taking baths with two younger sisters in our underpants. I never saw my father naked and only once when my sister and I helped our mother shower before she had nursing care did I see her undressed.

When I was ten, my parents registered for family swimming at the indoor pool in Great Neck High School on Sunday afternoons as part of a town program. Dressed in my bathing suit and rubber cap, I loved bobbing in the water on a cold winter day in the humid echo chamber that smelled of chlorine.

Afterwards in the cramped locker room, my sisters and I managed the technique of getting dressed while still wrapped in a towel as swaying breasts of the less modest moved like pendulums above our heads. Even the communal dressing rooms at Mays or Loehmann's hadn't prepared us for this fleshy display.

As a teen, private nakedness was another matter. With a flick of the experienced fingers of my steady boyfriend, my bra would be off and sometimes my panties around by ankles, but I wasn't totally bear with a man until I met my first husband. I had no problem with it, but I think I am more a voyeur than an exhibitionist.

I didn't see another male without clothing until two years after I was married when I was seated at the Broadway production of *Hair* in 1969. At the end of the performance, the audience was invited to join the naked cast on stage. Anonymity erased any inhibitions. And it was the Age of Aquarius. "I'm going up." I had focused on one amazing specimen in the cast line-up and found him on stage. We all joined hands and sang "Let the sun shine in." I leaned into him, "You are so hung."

He bent down and whispered, "Come backstage when this is over." Well, that was never going to happen. Plus I had to make a train back to suburbia, to my baby, and the only penis I would know for twenty plus years.

After divorcing in my late forties, I flew out to Colorado to spend the summer with Hedy, my favorite cousin, who was also single later in life. We took road trips in her truck and played at Thelma and Louise. On our way from Boulder to Telluride, we stopped in Ouray to meet her boyfriend, TJ, at Orvis Hot Springs nestled at the foot of the San Juan Mountains. They had arranged to rendezvous outside in the clothing optional area.

We walked through the wild flower gardens out back to the largest pool where Hedy and I were the only ones in bathing suits. There seemed to be mostly men. I tried to casually check out each one as I talked to Hedy, but it was hard to keep my eyes off an appendage that seemed to dangle a foot over the ledge of the outdoor pool.

We weren't there long before TJ showed up with a towel wrapped around his waist, which he removed after a brief introduction and then plunged into the pool. Hedy followed suit and asked me if I was going to join them.

"Yes, but I thought I would wait five minutes until I know TJ better." He humored me and listed his vital statistics and a brief bio. I slipped out of my suit and into the steamy water.

That night over beers at a friend's place in Telluride, TJ talked about the house he was helping his brother build and mentioned that the foundation was made out of bales of hay. Fascinated, I said they must be really, "*dick*." The word just hung in midair before I recovered, "I mean thick."

"Been a while?" he asked and we laughed and laughed.

I would see a lot of TJ on our five-day rafting trip on the Green River later that summer. He had a propensity to strip down naked while piloting his raft, raise his arms to the sky and roar, "I love the river."

I never got tired of it.

No Trespassing

Last week pimples were bumping out on the stems of the rosa rugosa, or saltspray rose, which ramble by the Ponquogue Bridge. Now I am happy to see the first pink floppy flowers with yellow stamens. The red-winged black birds that hang out in the marshy grass area have made their debut. Darting like a fluorescent butterfly, I spy my first windsurfer of the season. Firsts in general are often notable and sometimes, like first love, unforgettable.

A dark Irishman, the son of a cop and an Arthur Murray dance instructor, was the first to claim my heart. Sean and I met at a dance at the Bayside Yacht Club. Tall and handsome with shyness in his smiling eyes, he held my hand and walked me onto the dance floor. He taught me the Savoy, which is similar to the Lindy Hop. We went steady from sophomore year in high school to sophomore year in college. Before he had a driver's license, he took a bus or train to my neighborhood in Great Neck and walked the additional mile.

We were Mr. and Mrs. High School, the first couple on the dance floor at parties. At my senior prom the gym had been transformed into Camelot. We were chosen King and Queen by default, since the first two girls whose names were drawn had already left.

Since I was Sean's girl, I was welcome to hang out with the guys, mostly sons of cops and firemen who treated me like a person instead of a girl. I don't have any brothers; Sean and his friends were my introduction to the world of men.

He called me Gray; I called him Gallagher. When we were alone, I was dove, a blend of love and dear. During the week we were on the phone every night, and weekends ended with our bodies locked together at a train station or in a car.

We survived one year apart while I was at college in Philadelphia. Our letters, the highlight of my day, stretched thin across the miles before we broke up during the Christmas vacation of my sophomore year, a graveyard for the hometown boyfriends.

After midnight mass we sat on the carpeted floor in my parent's living room with just the twinkle of the Christmas tree lights. I had hidden his present, a guitar, under the couch. I slide it out and whispered, "Merry Christmas." He cradled it in his arms, strummed and sang "The Sloop John B." "I feel so broke up I just want to go home." He knew.

I can still picture us at the end of the vacation. We drove to our favorite diner and parked in the back lot. After an hour we walked inside to a booth by the window and sat watching the falling snow. It wasn't the pretty white fluffy stuff but a slushy mix of rain and sleet. Sean sat across from me hunched over the coffee neither of us drank. Neither of us talked. All our words were suspended inside his '56 Chevy. When the Righteous Brothers wailed "You've Lost that Loving Feeling" over the juke box we both broke down and cried. To this day I feel a pang when I hear that song.

It basically came down to a long distance relationship and the fact that Sean, a Catholic, only wanted to marry a virgin. Back in the early 60s, before the pill was the norm, girls were categorized as either tramps or the marrying kind. Heavy petting for another four years was too frustrating. And there was the parent factor. Sean wasn't initially college bound. My parents were afraid we would run off and get married. Their ultimate threat was that if we did, we'd live in an apartment above a store, which kind of appealed to me.

Just five years later, I was married to Jack with two children and living in Hampton Bays. Around that time Sean invested in a summer house a few blocks away. He and his friends frequented the same beach and bars that I did. After I saw him for the first time at Charlie Brown's, a local pub, my cousin said, "You look like you have just seen your best friend."

"Sean's here."

He was at Tiana Beach one day when I showed up. Friends watched my children while Sean and I sat on the ledge of a small cliff the outgoing tide had created. I sifted sand through my fingers while we tried to fill in the gap in our lives. He wanted to know about my *first time* since it was something we had thought would be ours.

That July my husband, Jack, and I were at one of our haunts. Sean was there too. On the way home Jack broke the silence, "You still love him."

"He was my growing up love; you are my grown-up love." But I didn't feel very grown up at 23.

Sean said that he would be out on weekends in the fall. Every Saturday and Sunday I drove down to Tiana Beach hoping to see his car. But by the end of September there had been no sign of him. I felt as empty and desolate as a winter beach. The next summer he showed up on the scene with his future wife, who tolerated our history.

After they were married my former love and his wife moved to Garden City and bought a house on the block behind my parents' home. By that time they had moved, but three of my sisters still lived in town. When I asked, they would share updates on Sean and his family. He eventually joined the same clubs we had belonged to and maintained a handicap that my father would have envied at the Garden City's Men's Club.

Whenever I visited my family, I would drive by our childhood home and then turn the corner and coast past his house. I was at my sister's for Easter weekend after I was divorced. In the morning I went jogging and found myself on the familiar route naming former neighbors as I passed their groomed gardens and seasonally decorated houses. I slowed down at number 92 and mentally hugged the Dutch colonial where I used to live, kind of expecting it to wink at me. I wondered how it could be inanimate when it held so many memories, like a well-maintained matron with no evidence of all that had gone on inside.

Before I knew it I was running down Sean's block. I was so busy looking at his Tudor style home, his tidy property, his antique car that I didn't notice the uneven pavement and went flying, landing spread eagle in front of his house. Madly muttering, "Please God don't let anything be broken." I envisioned myself having to do a commando crawl around the corner for help. Suddenly I realized a more urgent situation and cried, "Oh God don't let anyone see me."

I looked up and there might as well have been flashing neon "No Trespassing" sign on the front door. With stigmata on both hands and bleeding knees, I gingerly pulled myself together and limped the two miles back to my sister's.

❖ ❖ ❖ ❖ ❖

This incident was on my mind walking home from the bridge today. When I passed the Coast Guard Station, the two metal gates topped with barbed wire had just closed. They are covered with plaques: "Warning," "No Trespassing" and a large octagonal STOP sign. I nodded my head. I got the message.

The Tables Turn

The tide is going out. The magic of the morning light on Shinnecock Bay is long gone, and it's too early for the sunset display. Everything seems very clear at this hour on my daily walk across the Ponquogue Bridge.

For most of my life I had traveled on the straight and narrow path, but I took a detour when my two children were off at college. I eventually reached the final intersection and had to make a decision. With a soul in need of intensive care, it took me three years to close the door on a good man and 25 years of marriage.

Turning single in my late forties was like sailing without channel makers or charts. The next six years I felt lost many times, but a friend reminded me regularly that at least my life wasn't boring. I didn't miss being married, but I wanted a true partner who would navigate life with me.

At the top of the Bridge, I notice two kayakers skimming across the bay like dragonflies, and it reminds me of the night I met Mark. In the summer the Group for the East End sponsors a sunset moonrise paddle on Sagaponack Pond that ends at the barrier beach where a seasonal feast is served. I had gone the previous year and zigzagged across the water with friends. We had a great time and planned to do it again but no one was available. So I decided to go by myself.

What are the chances that I would park behind a Jeep with two women and three men who asked me to join them? What are the chances that I would end up in a kayak with a man I had never met who rented a house a mile from mine? Synchronicity was a new word in my vocabulary. I was constantly looking for signs. This seemed major.

Mark took charge, and we were off. Since I was in the bow of the forest green kayak, I had to turn around to steal quick glances: cute, short, in shape, good hair, and trimmed beard. We paddled well together, another sign, and then he began to sing "Lemon Tree." Actually the choice was prophetic, but all I could think was wow he's singing. We both marveled at the idyllic setting, admiring the same Post Modern houses that graced the shoreline.

After we landed I cornered one of the women he had arrived with and asked, "What's the story with Mark? Is he married, divorced, gay?" She replied that he had lived with her sister years ago, but that he never married. She added if I wanted more than good company, he wasn't the guy.

Instead of letting that sink in, I thought he couldn't be a creep if they were still friends with him. But he was 49 and had never been married, which was a minus in my book, but how romantic would it be if a confirmed bachelor fell for me. It would make a great write-up in the Vows section of the Sunday New York Times.

It was a perfect night with all the elements co-operating. I sat in a semi-circle with Mark and his friends for cocktails followed by dinner. We stood on line to be served freshly caught striped bass, hot off the grill. Then we helped ourselves to slices of Black Krim, Amana Orange and Grandma Oliver's heirloom tomatoes layered between basil and mozzarella. I made room on my plate for roasted sweet corn, glistening with butter, and ice cold watermelon. The kind of food you dream about in the winter.

After dinner we walked on the beach. When the drummers started a rhythmic chant coaxing the moon to rise, Mark and I started to dance. Gyrating to the primitive beat thumping in our chests and vibrating through our bodies, we hailed the rising orb. A huge moon dripping pink rose over the glassy swells. I felt reckless abandon and wanted to rip my clothes off and run naked. Mark brushed the hair away from my face and kissed me. By the end of the night I was 'babe.' He took my number. I knew he would call.

The truth of our relationship was that it was more booty call than dating. Saturday night dates were rare. But it was convenient to have a male friend down the block, "Denise, how about a cocktail?"

We were compatible. He'd begin conversations with, "Tell me about your day." And like a wind-up doll I'd go on and on, and he would listen. The fact that he was an artist appealed to me; he appreciated my praise and critique. We had fun, but like moons in different phases, we didn't fit together.

On Good Friday, Mark called and asked if I wanted to walk across the Ponquogue Bridge. A stiff southerly wind whipped off a percolating ocean, so we walked with our heads bent against the gusts staring at the charcoal grey mudflats below.

On the way back the gale was behind us. It seemed to inflate my jacket like a kite ready to rise. I blurted out, "Mark, I'm confused about us. I know we enjoy each other's company. Why can't we be a real couple? It's frustrating me. What's the story Mark? Is it you? Is it me?

"You wanna know?"

"Yes, I want to know."

"You want the truth?"

"Yeah. I do"

"Okay. I want a 35-year-old with a tight ass."

I was speechless. I was too busy calculating whether I could throw him off the bridge. He wasn't a big man. Then I started to argue.

"Does this mean you want a family?"

"Not necessarily."

"But Mark, most 35-year-old women already have a family or are anxious to start one." I refrained from yelling what makes you think that a young woman would want a short, self-centered 50-year-old man who's neither rich nor great looking. But I refrained. As we neared the driveway, I think it might have dawned on him that he had hurt my feelings.

"Denise, doesn't everyone want a young tush?"

"No. I think you're fine."

"But I have a tight ass."

"No, Mark, you *are* a tight ass." I left him staring at the gravel.

Since my divorce I felt more or less ageless although the mirror confirmed the truth. But I was in good shape, and I truly celebrated turning fifty. When I was in my forties, my first lover was six years younger. When we discussed our age difference, he said that he'd love me even if I was 50. If all men felt this way, I was at the end of my love life, a perennial wallflower.

If I had been crucified on Friday, I rose from the dead on Sunday. The next guy who saw my ass was going to love it. If a man was so shallow that he was more interested in an age than a person, I didn't want him anyway.

About a month later, I chaperoned a five-day trip to Frost Valley. On day one, during a tour of the grounds, I found myself walking next to a divorced father, a darling fireman. Despite the fact that I was an older woman, by good decade, we hit it off immediately. By the end of the day we had made a date to kayak. For a year he kept his boat in my yard. He loved my ass; I loved that he was 38.

Open Door

A herring gull with the orange dot on its beak sits on the edge of the bridge this morning. Each time I get closer, it moves a few feet away. After the third time it spreads its wings and takes off.

I thought, that's how many times it took me to close the revolving door with Mark. Our relationship started up again each time he moved to a new rental property. He never owned a house. We'd run into each on the streets of Bridgehampton or Sag Harbor. We'd have a cocktail, and one thing would lead to the next. The last time we were together was the summer he leased a condo in Vermont.

Because I knew it wouldn't last, I appreciated the crispness of the July morning as I drove past the Tastee Freez and the hollyhock-trimmed hardware store with Flexible Flyers in the window. I stopped at the all purpose gas station to fill up an empty tank before I left another man and Vermont behind. My visit with Mark ended sadly, with him drinking vodka straight up at lunch to paralyze any vulnerability, to drown any meaningful words, to numb any feelings.

When I passed the state line leaving Vermont in the rear-view mirror, I started to cry. Why do I keep putting myself in this position? Why do I expect more from Mark than he can or wants to give? Why can't I just accept this for what it is?

Somewhere in Massachusetts my Volvo started to lose power. The speedometer would drop from 70 mph to 50 and then recover. I was hoping it was just a freak thing, but it happened again twenty miles down the highway. I decided to move into the slow lane. Reluctantly I turned off the air conditioning because I thought it might be draining energy. As a last resort I shut the radio off too. But the problem got worse dropping to 40 mph and jerking back up to 50

As I approached the Verrazano Bridge, I was on the verge of hysterics. If I broke down on the bridge maybe it would be better to just jump than wait to be hit by oncoming traffic. The way I was feeling it seemed like the right thing to do. I took a deep breath, gripped the steering wheel and prayed. I made it across, but the stalling incidents became much more frequent. When I started to slow down on the Cross Island Expressway, I pulled onto the shoulder and merged back when the power revived.

Finally, I got off at the Glen Cove exit close to Garden City where three of my sisters lived. No one was home. By the time I called AAA, I was babbling like an idiot. A tow truck arrived in record time.

A wiry mechanic bopped over to my car. "Hi. How's it going?"

I sobbed, "I'm so fucking hot I can't think straight. I just broke up with my boyfriend, and my mother is dying of cancer."

Silence.

I though, another stupid man who can't talk.

"Jump in. We don't have far to go."

I sat slumped in the square box of an office. The desk was littered with 7-Eleven coffee cups and paper-work; the expected pin-up calendar was on the cinder block wall. My bare legs stuck to the green plastic covered chair. When my mental mouth finally shut, I tuned into a buzzing sound. There was an enormous bumble bee careening into the corners of the room looking for escape. Again and again she bounced along the wall. All along, the door was open.

It's True What They Say

Cumulus clouds take center stage on today's walk across the Ponquogue Bridge. The type that makes you want to lie on your back and watch as the shape of a castle morphs into a dragon. I scan the sky trying to see the eye socket of a Georgica O'Keefe skeleton or maybe just a puppy, but it's not happening. I'm trying too hard, kind of like looking for Mr. Right. When I was single at 50 and expecting every guy I met to be the one, wiser folks would sing song it will happen when you least expect it. They were right. I parroted this message to my younger sister after she got divorced.

Laura aka Lolo, Laurette, Lucy is the middle child in a series of five girls in seven years. She and her first husband moved to Boston after they were married. When Laura became pregnant and Robby was between jobs, they came back to New York where my father hired his son-in-law. Eventually he became the vice president of my father's company. This enabled him to enjoy a very high lifestyle that ended in a downward spiral.

His job and then his marriage were terminated in the late nineties. It was a very hard time for Laura playing monkey in the middle of her father and her husband.

Whenever I called her after the split, she didn't bash her ex or complain about moving from an impressive Tudor to a third floor walk-up apartment in the same town. She just cried, "I am so lonely. I can't stand it. I hate to be alone."

Not long after, our sister Suzan left her husband of twenty-five years for Jim, her high school sweetheart. They were engaged when she was 19. My parents were not happy about it and that put a strain on the young love; eventually they broke up. Sue and Jim connected later in life through the internet. Until her divorce was final and money available, she moved in with Laura. The situation worked well for them initially. Laura was desperate for company, and Suzan needed a place to stay.

However, of the five Gray sisters they are the most unlikely duo. Even physically they are different. We always teased Suzan that she was the adopted one because she doesn't resemble the rest of us.

She is the tallest, with an athletic build, blonde with beautiful generous features that haven't aged like the rest of us. In her younger years Laura had an Elizabeth Taylor look. Now she has a flair for big hats and has been known to wear one of those T shirts with a picture of sexy body.

Their personalities are as different as their looks. Self-contained, Suzan's emails are terse, shortened with abbreviated words and generally with the logo of the real estate company she works for. Laura's long emails are heavy with capital letters, OMGs and explanation points. Suzan, who is two years older than Laura, is content with her knitting needles, decorating books and magazines. With daytime TV as a constant companion, Laura creates the most thoughtful birthday cards filled with glitter, an old photo and your horoscope.

A certified interior designer, Suzan advised Laura, on a few sophisticated decorating choices. Later in life Laura would turn her living room into a fairyland for her four granddaughters complete with a beautiful tepee and activity centers that would rival any nursery school.

Despite their differences, they enjoyed being roommates. Suzan is an attentive listener, and Laura, who has Rose Ann Barr's humor, loves an audience. Both are gifted mimics; together they laughed a lot.

Suzan also helped her roommate move from a two bedroom into a one bedroom apartment. This meant that Suzan slept on a blow-up mattress that disappeared early in the morning. Although they had fun with each other, it bothered Laura that Suzan was constantly on the phone with Jim. This often led Laura to retreat into her room where she felt more alone because she didn't have a serious love at the time.

After a year of cohabitating, Suzan moved to Florida to be with Jim. Laura could not stop repeating, "I am so glad to be alone."

Shortly after, Laura met Paul at a friend's New Year's Eve party where they discovered their mutual love of champagne. Paul had never been married, but Laura was not deterred. A year later they tied the knot in a helicopter over Niagara Falls on her 60th birthday.

Someday Came

Fishing on Shinnecock Bay is winding down at this hour approaching sunset. I stand at the top of the Ponquogue Bridge straining to read the names of the boats as they rush through the channel leaving silver wakes unfurled like show girls' feathers. Some of them are so clever: *Fishful Thinking, Teak for Two, Someday Came.* I think yes. Yes, it did as I hum Walt Disney's "Someday my Prince Will Come."

Who knows a woman better than her hairdresser? Joseph and I have been sharing secrets for more than twenty years. During one of my appointments he invited me to a party. At first I said no because I was going into the city and wouldn't be home until early evening. But Joseph persisted. He explained that a group from the gym was getting together, and they had asked this guy Terry to join them. When they suggested he bring a date, Terry said he wasn't seeing anyone. Joseph claimed a light bulb went off in his head, and he blurted out my name.

I had been divorced for six years. This was the first time Joseph had tried to fix me up. I asked for details. He recited lean and muscled, Irish, good head of white hair, handsome, a widower.

Terence Patrick Meehan was all that and more. While a party whirled around us, we sat at a well-worn kitchen table and talked. Actually he did most of the talking which I read in my self-help books when I got home was like a rooster strutting his stuff. I was impressed that he had finished college in his forties. At twenty he had dropped out of Iona College and joined the Marines Corps back in the Vietnam era.

After the party, which was located in a suburban maze, ended I wasn't sure how to find my way back to Sunrise Highway. Terry suggested that I follow him. Cool as the November night, he slid into his teal blue Camaro, convertible top still down. But he never said good-bye or asked for my number. Like the snowy white egret standing on the rocks with a drainpipe neck extended, I guessed he didn't want to get his feet wet.

When I returned to the salon, Joseph waving his arms yelled, "Denise, Terry has been asking for your number. I've been putting him off because I wasn't sure if you were interested."

"Yeah, definitely. Give him my number."

Our first date was dinner at a hamburger place. I remember the creases along the sleeves of his light grey sweater showed how carefully he had dressed. It seemed to me that he had two different faces; his smile totally transformed him. I sensed he was not a simple study.

I filed the little things he mentioned into my memory. He doesn't like his nails dirty or his hair mussed. I thought maybe opposites do attract. I am a gardener who rarely uses a hairdryer and often prefers my fingers to a comb. He shared that his three children had given him a card on Mother's Day as well as Father's Day. I thought this guy is solid.

At the end of the night, Terry approached our first kiss as awkwardly as a boy in the movie theater pretending to yawn and stretch as an excuse to get his arm around a girl. One day I came home to find a new strainer for my kitchen sink hanging on my front door. Terry knew mine was broken. Some things are better than flowers.

On our second date, a photography exhibit followed by dinner, Terry and I began filling in the spaces of our lives with blanket information and then slowly pulling back the covers. He talked about his deceased wife, who died of an enlarged heart ten years earlier when she was thirty-six and he was forty-two. He described the ups and downs of their marriage. I shared the demise of my mine as well as an outline of my life as a divorced woman.

On our third date my romantic man arrived with a pot of rich beef stew, a loaf of bread and a bottle of red wine. Later he stroked my head and read Robert Graves' poem "Symptoms of Love."

"Love is a universal migraine...Take courage, lover! Could you endure such pain at any hand but hers?"

And I knew he was ready to take the plunge.

Angel

On this morning's walk I observe that the twigs reaching beyond the bridge railing look like witches' fingers. A banner advertising the play "Wicked" trails behind a plane that seems to be just hanging like a star. My stepdaughter calls me the wicked stepmother, mostly in jest. Beth, Terry's youngest, was eleven when her mother died.

I am a jealous, possessive woman. Having an ex around would have been challenging. It was fortunate for me that my husband Terry was a widower when we met in our fifties. His wife Hedy died of an enlarged heart in her mid-thirties leaving Terry with three children: David, Terence and Beth. In the beginning of the courtship game, when you show your best suit, Terry's ace was that his kids used to give him Mother's Day cards.

On our second date we finessed around some of the more complex issues of our marriages and mates. Terry talked about his first wife, whom he had met in the housing projects in Manhattan where he grew up.

I perked up at the mention of her name, Hedy. One you don't hear very often. My cousin Hedy, a fixture in my childhood and a true friend throughout my life, shares the same name. She happened to call from her home in Colorado that week. At the end of our conversation she asked, "Did you hear that Hedy Lamarr died?" I took these to be signs that I would be haunted, in a good way, by the late Mrs. Meehan

When we repeated these coincidences to the minister who would marry us, his genial face grew pale. His wife had passed away recently; her name was Hedy. I started to think of Hedy Meehan as a friendly ghost. Later I decided she was more like an angel, someone definitely on my side.

When Terry and I were dating, his three children were in their twenties. Lucky for all of us. Raising teenagers in an established marriage is hard enough. His children's approval was important to me; I think Hedy paved the way. Maybe she knew I would always honor her memory and that I had no intention of taking her place. I love her children's father, and I hoped to be someone her kids could count on.

❖❖❖❖❖

Beth is the closest to her father, and the one I thought I might have a problem with since she is the baby of the family as well as the only girl. When I met her for the first time, I was sitting on the floral couch in their living room leafing through a magazine waiting for her father to come home. She and friend entered the front door laughing. I stood up, "You must be Beth."

"Hi, Denise." Beth immediately drew me into their conversation. It was as if she knew me. She was easy to love.

A few years later I gave Beth a generous gift toward her wedding gown. I arrived at the bridal salon and cried when she parted the dressing room curtains and stepped onto the platform before the mirrors. She was breathtaking with jet black hair, the tan complexion of her Argentine mother, a few freckles and the little lips of her Irish father.

Beth's husband, Heath, likes to say, "She has the toughness of the Irish, the drama of the Latin blood and I am screwed."

I didn't know the word comped until I met Beth. After her reception there was a problem at the hotel where several of the rooms we had reserved were not available. She stood at the registration desk in her wedding gown and negotiated a deal to be compensated for our inconvenience. It included rooms at a reduced price in a neighboring hotel and complimentary breakfast for all her guests. Terry attributed Beth's persuasive persistence to her mother, Hedy.

Hedy's family tradition of Argentine meat pies is enjoyed by our family now. They are labor intensive. Chopped meat, raisins, olives and secret ingredients are sautéed and then stuffed into the wrappers, sealed and crimped in a press and then fried. I encouraged Beth to switch from Entenmann's to empanadas. When she presented her first platter of empanadas, Beth graduated from girl to woman.

Four years ago Beth's only child, Jayden, made the evening news. He was running with a small American flag in his hand when he tripped. As he fell with his mouth open, the wooden stick on the flag became impaled in the soft tissue at the back of his mouth. Beth raced him to Peconic Bay Hospital in Riverhead. We met her there. Four-year-old Jayden sat in the hospital bed, eyes wide with the red, white and blue fabric of the American flag sticking out of his mouth.

Because of several potentially life-threatening possibilities, he was transferred by ambulance to Stony Brook Hospital, a familiar place to us since he had spent the first month of his life there as an under-three-pound preemie. After a tortuous wait, the flag was surgically removed. Jayden was running around the next day.

At midnight Beth and Heath walked with us down to the empty lobby. Resting my head on her shoulder I hugged her tightly, "You know that it's no coincidence that your gynecologist, pediatrician and babysitter are all Argentine. It's good to have an angel, Beth."

❖ ❖ ❖ ❖ ❖

I had been warned that Terry's son, David, was the deal breaker. On his bedside table is a framed picture of his mother, Hedy: long dark hair, full faced, unsmiling. He hadn't liked the woman his father was seriously involved with a few years before me, or maybe it wasn't the woman but the idea of his father and another woman. He had made his feelings known, and the relationship did not survive. So I was nervous about meeting him. But the timing was right; I was right and got the nod from David, our future best man.

Even listening to David's greeting on his cell phone makes him instantly likeable. He has a posse of friends who call him Mr. GQ. I call him Mr. Clean. I know that before everyone leaves on Christmas Eve the playroom will be in alphabetical order. He takes his role of first born seriously. Despite Beth's protests, David tries to be the boss of her. His brother Terence's voice changes when he talks to his older brother on the phone.

David's daughter Gabrielle, talks about her talent: singing. A year ago when she was eight she started singing and piano lessons. I always thought that she had a terrific voice, but after her first recital I feel she is destined to be on stage. It was held in a church. Gabrielle walked up the aisle, took that microphone in her hands, looked up and "These Are a Few of My Favorite Things" filled the chapel.

The next recital was a formal setting with a stage. Gabrielle, dressed in a dark navy dress with her raven hair falling around her shoulders, was a star. David just lost it. Kneeling behind the last row he balled his eyes out. I can only assume that he saw his mother's face and heard her voice in his daughter.

❖❖❖❖❖

Terence was at Harvard working on his masters at the Kennedy School of Government when I met Terry. After we had been dating a few months, we drove up to Boston to visit him. He met us with a friend at a seafood restaurant where the food was awful, but the company made the meal unimportant. On our way home as Terence and his long- time boyfriend strolled shoulder to shoulder down Tremont Street I said to Terry, "Terence is gay. Why didn't you tell me?"

"I wanted you to think of him as Terence, not just as the gay son.

Terry's children, except for Terence, rarely talk about their mother. I don't think it's in deference to me, they just don't, but I do. Terence, who shares similar views about spirituality with me, came for a visit when he was going through a difficult time. I thought walking the beach might help to air out his mind. When we were driving across the Ponquogue Bridge, a seagull flew at eye level with Terence the entire length of the span. We just looked at each other. I said, "You know your mother is always with you."

When Terence graduated from Harvard he chose a restaurant called Hedy's for his celebration. He will be attending medical school this year.

❖❖❖❖❖

My children, who love Terry, saw my time being divided by five instead of two. It took time. We worked out holiday schedules and hosted family dinners. One Easter my daughter Melissa popped into the kitchen and out of the blue announced, "I really like my step-sibs." My son sees our gatherings as a party.

Terry and I were at the hospital for the births of our grandchildren. Becoming Mim sealed my

status in the family. In my mind there is no such thing as step-grandchildren. So we are not the Brady Bunch, but we are a blended family.

9/11

A thick vine of bittersweet is rooted by the railing where I park my car at the Ponquogue Bridge. The leaves have started turning color, but the berries haven't burst out of their yellow jackets yet exposing red bellies.

It's a beautiful day, the kind we have come to associate with 9/11. I wonder if it is a comfort to the families of the 9/11 victims. Do blue skies and the warmth of the sun help to lift their spirits? Or are they pissed off that this day can seem so normal, that the world is still spinning on its axis, when for some, the center of their world is gone?

The few people on the bridge walk with their heads bowed. The cement memorial benches below are all empty. I think about the empty seats left by the nearly 2,750 people lost in the Twin Towers: the seat at the head of the dining room table, the recliner in front of the TV, the stool at the neighborhood bar, the swivel chair at an office desk.

That morning my son, Ashley, called from his Park Place office 150 yards from the Twin Towers. "Mom, are you watching the news?"

"No, I just got in from a walk. What's going on Ash?" I asked as I placed my sunglasses and water bottle on the foyer table.

"You're not going to believe it. A plane crashed into the World Trade Center a few minutes ago."

"You're kidding. What kind of plane?" I was thinking probably some stunt gone awry as I picked up the newspaper and walked into the kitchen.

"I don't know. It's pandemonium around here."

"Probably some idiot."

"Got to go, Mom. I'll call you later."

"Okay honey. I'll turn on the TV and check it out." I ended our conversation the way I always do, "I love you, Ash."

"Love you too."

I headed to our outdoor shower. The phone was ringing as I stepped back into the house. It was my sister Jennifer. "Have you heard from Ashley?"

Still wrapped in a towel I answered, "Yeah, he called twenty minutes ago."

"Turn on the TV, Den. A second plane has attacked the towers."

For the next few hours I sat riveted to the television set with the phone on my lap, my lips moving in silent prayer. Finally a friend of Ashley's was able to get a message to me that my only son was okay and making his way home.

I could barely contain myself. I pushed open the screen door, fell into the backyard, and began ripping down invading wisteria vines that I had allowed to encroach during the summer. I pulled up weeds and yanked up Black Eyed Susans and Queen Anne's lace that had sprouted where they didn't belong.

Late in the afternoon I heard a car door slam and Ashley sprinted through the open gate and into my arms. I cried, "Oh God Ash."

"I ran as fast as I could for as long as I could."

"How did you get home?"

"I was on the 59th Street Bridge with a guy from Manhasset when a limo driver pulled up and asked if we wanted a ride."

"That was lucky."

"The chauffeur's boss lives in Manhasset. He dropped off my friend and then took me to the Ronkonkoma Train Station. He paused and choked, "That train. Dead quiet."

Too soon for so many stories.

Later he told me that when the first plane struck it was the loudest sound he had ever heard. Two of the older men in his office immediately ran out of the building. Looking back he remembered that they had survived the first attack on the Trade Center in 1993. Ashley and his co-workers filed outside to see a gaping hole in the side of Tower 1. They began to realize that the specks falling from the sky were people, possibly people they knew.

And he ran.

Standing at the Washington Square Archway, he saw the second tower fall. No one thought the building would collapse into a pancake.

My son lives in the city but spends a majority of his weekends at his home in our town, so we see him often. I hadn't visited his apartment on Murray Street or been to his office around the corner. I knew he lived close to the disaster, but it wasn't until several years after 9/11 that I felt I could handle seeing how close. The top of his office building had been sheared off and the business relocated for months.

It was a May morning bright with spring when I took the train into the city to spend an overnight at Ashley's apartment and to see the remains of the World Trade Center. I walked to the site he passed every day. The scene was like a war zone: a massive hole, wire fences and names on temporary panels. My first cousin Jimmy Smith, father of four; my cousin's son Matthew Vianna, only 23, Art Jones and Jack "Axe" Mc Dougal, two men who had grown up with my children; family names from Garden City, where my sisters lived, and Manhasset, where I went to high school. So many.

Before I returned to the Hamptons, I decided to walk the Brooklyn Bridge. I was looking for exercise so I started off with a brisk pace, but I found myself slowing down and actually sitting on a bench while life swirled around me. The pedestrian traffic was heavy with foreign accents, women in business attire and sneakers, children in two straight lines holding their partners' hands. On the way back to Manhattan I looked over the slate gray river at the space where the twin towers should have been and then at the Statue of Liberty.

I wanted to yell, "Drop your torch and raise your fist."

Angel On My Side

Terry and I were married the Sunday after 9/11. My eyes were swollen from crying most of the week. I lost two cousins in the attack. We had thought about postponing our ceremony, but we were reassured that a life-affirming celebration was needed. Besides the horror and aftermath of 9/11, and the normal wedding stress, Terry and I were embroiled in our first fight.

The problem was with the in-laws: Terry's deceased wife Hedy's family. My introduction to them was at his son David's first wedding. I was standing outside the stone church with Terry's mother, Dot, when an imposing woman slinked towards us. Dot leaned in, "Ida, Hedy's mother." I had been warned. Draped in a full length mink coat and oversized sunglasses she greeted Dot and then asked if I was her daughter.

I said. "No, I'm Denise. I'm with Terry."

"Terry who?" And she walked away.

Sliding into the church pew, I whispered to Terry, "I met Ida" and relayed our short conversation.

He said, "I'm dead to her," an expression I had never heard. "Tell you later."

At the reception I watched her. She looked like an old movie star in a carefully coifed wig and a long gold mesh dress stretched over her reed-thin body. But more mesmerizing than her appearance were her camera-ready poses and postures.

Coming back from the dance floor I passed behind her chair and under her breath she snarled, "Fucking bitch." Years later Ida did not come to her granddaughter Beth's wedding because I would be there as Terry's wife. Beth took my side and the gulf widened, never to be crossed. In between courses and during a few slow dances, Terry tried to explain the family dynamics. He and Hedy had moved out of the city to get away from her family. After Hedy died her mother, Ida, had irrational thoughts about Terry never remarrying. These are troubled people who make trouble.

Back in our hotel room lying in bed after the reception, Terry was more quiet than usual. Some of the joy, that love hangover after a wedding, was missing. 'It must have been bittersweet for you today. It's sad to me that Hedy wasn't there is see her son married."

Terry rolled over and faced me, "I am glad you were with me."

"I am afraid that you miss the Latin beauties and the drama."

"We moved to Long Island to get away from that drama. I don't want it. I don't need it. You are my Irish beauty. I have had the best of both worlds."

Words I needed to hear.

When Terry and I were planning our wedding, we had asked his children if they wanted anyone in Hedy's family included. I held my breath. Fortunately, they decided that it wasn't appropriate. Since Terry had been officially dead to Ida for years anyway, I didn't think she would want to come. But Janet, his former sister-in-law, kept putting pressure on her niece and nephews trying to wheedle her way in. I knew this woman could single-handedly destroy our day. I was furious that Terry was even entertaining these conversations.

Punching doors didn't help, words only fueled the fire and then my heart stepped in. It wasn't anger it was fear. Fear that my husband would be other people's hero not mine. Fear he was more attracted to dark-skinned women, and I am white bread. Fear that his attractive, conniving sister-in-law would take over the dance floor, and my wedding would become about her. I could not compete.

I tried to see Terry through the lens of love rather than my insecurity. I came to realize that his role in the family was to keep the peace. He was doing the best he could. First, I got in touch with the woman who would be playing music at our reception. I told her that if anyone requested Latin music to nod but never, never play it.

Then I called Terry and said that I could deal with whatever he decided. At the same time he told me that he had spoken to his children's aunt and made it clear that she was not invited. I can't help but think that Hedy understood my situation and whispered in his ear.

Span 20

Nest 2

The Ospreys are back.

I checked the NY Birding list, and the first sighting of the osprey, or fish hawk, this year was the last day of March. Yesterday I drove by an osprey's nest, a McMansion, on the corner of Flanders Road and Route 105 in Riverhead. I was excited to see it was occupied. On a mission this morning, I scan the marsh grass to a nest atop a slanted pole. Sure enough, an adult osprey is posted on its rim.

After the divorce my nest was a source of comfort and security. I saw my house as more than just a home but a means to an end. I needed money, so I rented it for several summers. The money enabled me to pay my share of our daughter's wedding, get out of debt and make some home improvements. I had ceiling fans installed in all the rooms, a window and single door in the family room were replaced with French doors, and I expanded the upper deck, which provided shade on the lower deck.

In January of the new millennium, I had my first date with my husband Terry, a widower, who is a fan of ospreys and knows the location of many of their nests. A year later when Terry and I got married, we talked about selling the house and buying or building one together. At the time, to replace what we had would have cost us a lot more money. Besides, I think Terry really understood how important my home was to me.

Over the years, Terry has changed the house that Jack built to make it his. The third bedroom was his first renovation. He decided I needed a room of my own where I could write. We added beautiful crown molding and built-in bookcases. When the project was complete, I opened the door for the inspection. There on the center of my new desk was a sleek laptop, my first.

I was the general contractor for the next project: the master bedroom and bath. I like to say that I had great help except for the cute Irishman named Terry who was so slow. My husband can't change a light bulb without going down to the studs.

The day before our first Easter dinner with our combined families, I was at an estate sale in Bridgehampton. Standing at the doorway of the loft-like room, I zeroed in on the dining room table fully extended with leaves at either end. I pictured our five children and their mates gathered around it with room to grow. Besides its size, I loved the richness of the maple wood and the craftsman feeling that there isn't another one like it.

❖❖❖❖❖

A robin red breast springs around the front lawn as I drag myself down my driveway. I'm tired after today's walk. In the flower bed tulip tips like baby teeth break through the ground and daylilies' tongues start to green balding patches. I look at my front door and think I am glad to be home.

Before Terry's house was sold, we divided our time between his and mine. I told him that home was wherever he is. The grey saltbox by the dead end sign on Shinnecock Road is our feathered nest where we have parties with our extended family, which now includes six grandchildren.

Holding Back the Tide

Looking down from the bridge, I see that the project along- side the bay is finished. A new, clean cement curb has replaced the crumbling one. The area has been repaved and tidy white t-shaped lines painted for parking spaces. It's a big improvement but probably temporary. Beyond the curb, past thinning layers of rocks, splintered pilings stand like a Jack o' Lantern's teeth.

This reflects my beliefs about facelifts. A close friend had one this spring. So I have been thinking about aging and trying to hold back the tide.

Even after cosmetic surgery morphed from something you associated with movie stars to something your neighbor had done, I had reservations about it. But, seven years ago I went under the knife for a small procedure. Before I made that decision, I cut through layers of concerns and history.

In my family, we worried more about our arms than our faces. Despite the fact that we are fairly petite, some of us have arms like ham hocks. I remember one hot summer when my seventy-year-old mother decided she could get away with wearing a white sleeveless top to a party. After the pictures arrived, she had second thoughts. I discovered my mother standing at the kitchen counter with scissors amputating her arms from the photos. She looked up at me, "What was I thinking?"

Her mother had sagging triceps that we called Irish Harps. My paternal grandmother's fleshy arms swayed like pendulums. My youngest sister, whose Botox treatments are as regular has her dental appointments, was horrified by our gene pool. She actually had liposuction in that area, which really made a difference until she stopped exercising and gained weight.

My mother didn't like her arms, but bragged that she had earned the lines etched into her heart-shaped face. However, when her ophthalmologist recommended having folds of skin on her eyelids removed, she toyed with the idea. I encouraged her, so I could see my future face. However, she never had it done because she was diagnosed with lung cancer and needed a different type of surgery.

Platitudes like "Beauty is only skin deep," and "Beauty is as beauty does," were pounded into my head by my mother and the nuns. I grew up in the age of the Noxzema scrubbed face, followed by the hippie stage. No makeup, a long braid and leotards with jeans or flowing skirts happened to fit my budget as a young mother. I didn't finish a tube of lipstick until I was forty.

However, vanity is hard to escape. Grey hair entered my life with the birth of my daughter when I was 22. I have been dyeing it for decades. I also wear makeup and use other products to enhance my appearance. Good grooming really counts when the glow of youth disappears, but I still felt surgery seemed to cross the line.

Plus there were other considerations. According to my sister cosmetic surgery is addictive. Another problem is after a while something else gives your age away. Discretionary income is another factor. If I had an extra $16,000, I'd rather rent a villa in Italy. Memories last longer than a facelift.

I realized that a facelift is probably not in my future, but as I approached sixty, a number that did not roll easily off my tongue; I started to think seriously about having my eyelids lifted.

After washing my face in the morning, it was often necessary to pull the excess skin from my eyelids up and back out of the way. It bothered me when people asked me if I was tired, when actually I felt peppy. My grandmother's words, "Denise, I'm just a young woman trapped in an old body." rang true. I pictured her face with crepey eyelids like venetian blinds and decided that I would have mine raised before I entered the next decade.

Like the perfect storm these factors combined. If sixty is the new forty, I wanted to appear younger and more rested. Secondly, I felt comfortable with my mother's ophthalmologist whose rates were reasonable if insurance didn't cover the blepharoplasty. He assured me that I was a perfect candidate. And, finally, my husband reassured me, "I'll love you droopy lids and all". Maybe the tipping point was the fact that he used the word droopy.

I preferred to think of it as vision improvement rather than a vanity issue. But I was terrified of a perpetual wide-eyed look of an animal surprised by headlights or the cat-woman effect. My doctor promised me a natural result.

Thanks to the valium I was instructed to take an hour before my appointment, the in-office procedure was a piece of cake. I was supposed to apply Bacitracin twice daily and to eat a lot of pineapple because it contains bromelain, a powerful enzyme that reduces inflammation. At first the stitches felt like sand in my eyes. By the third day, my eyes began to itch and to feel swollen.

Almost a week later, I visited a friend whose husband had had a blepharoplasty shortly before mine. He looked great. I complained that my eyes were bothering me. "Just keep using the ointment." So instead of twice a day, I doubled the dose. Two days later my face had ballooned to my jaw line, and my eyes were swollen shut.

My husband drove me to the emergency room. I guess because I looked like a Star Trek character I was admitted immediately. The doctor took one look at me, scanned my paperwork and stated, "Seems like you are allergic to the extended use of Bacitracin." After seven days of steroids I looked like myself, only better.

Despite the complications, the result was worth it. But how long will it last?

Endangered Species

I am fighting the fact that today is the first of August, the most serious summer month. Thirty-one days of last licks. I've been in the ocean only twice this season. So instead of walking the bridge, I decide to take my shoes off and stroll on the sand to the inlet and back.

At the east end of Ponquogue Beach an orange plastic fence marks the piping plovers' property. This section is reserved to protect their eggs, which are laid in shallow depressions, called scrapes, well above the high tide mark. These sparrow-sized birds, the color of dry sand, have the best real estate in town. We are taking such good care of them here on the East Coast that they are now threatened not endangered.

I consider myself an endangered species. I am a letter writer. After lists mailed to Santa Claus, missives to pen pals and thank you notes, I became a serious letter writer when I was a college freshman in Philadelphia. In 1963 long distance calls were saved for special occasions and emergencies. Every day before lunch, I checked my mail slot hoping to find letters from home. My high school boyfriend and I wrote to each other several times a week. Checks from my father would arrive with a short note "make it last" and signed with his signature smiley face wearing glasses.

After college graduation, I kept in touch with friends through letters. Maryland resident Sue Kaufman Codd and I wrote to each other for years. Through our letters, we knew the nitty gritty details of each others' lives. Our children were close in age, and we measured their progress, the things we loved about them, what drove us crazy.

In a competitive spirit, if she told me she had crocheted a granny square vest, I'd get my needle out and finish one so in my next letter I could describe mine. We shared the books we read, the movies we saw, and the dinner parties we hosted. There was no reading between the lines when it came to the disappointments in our lives.

Sue died in 2003. At a reception following her funeral, I could identify her friends from her vivid descriptions so long ago. I looked at them with knowing eyes; I knew their secrets. Sue and I thought someday we would publish our letters. A stack of them wrapped with ribbon addressed in her tiny perfect penmanship sits on a shelf in my office. I still haven't untied them.

Another dear college friend Mary Jo Barbi and I started the tradition of birthday letters to each other in addition to Christmas updates. After we advanced to email we promised to continue the tradition. In her most recent letter, she told me that she has multiple myeloma.

"...Not to awfulize the situation, but I've been busy planning my funeral. We have a plot by the river...a few tunes. Carly Simon, "Coming Around Again," the Stones, "Get Off My Cloud" and the Black Eyed Peas, "Tonight's the Night." Mimosas of course...no priest...no church..."

I wrote back, "... I can understand planning your funeral. I would do the same. My ashes thrown from the Ponquogue Bridge and a party at the beach. I like your music selections. Bagpipes would be on my list and a drunken rendition of Randy and the Rainbow's "Denise Denise"..."

❖❖❖❖❖

In the 1980s my parents decided to sell their big house and spend half the year in Florida and the other in Hampton Bays. I walked into the kitchen and found my mother crying surrounded by packing crates.

"Mom, I thought you were happy about this move."

"I am, but I am throwing away my daughters' memories."

Glancing around I noticed yearbooks, warped record albums and pink prom dresses that propped up budding breasts. Peering into a carton I caught my breath. I stroked the Bass Weejun shoe box I knew was filled with letters from my first love. I couldn't take them with me when I got married, but I couldn't throw them away. So I left them in my mother's attic.

When I was angry or hurt by my children they got The Letter. My son, Ashley, used to read them to his roommates. They particularly liked the ones about good manners. Now he sends me humorous cards and texts with pictures of his baby, Sailor Marie. One of the best things about my daughter, Melissa, going away to college was that we wrote to each other. Later in life both of my children gifted me with the sweetest appreciative notes.

My husband Terry has the uncanny knack of selecting the best Hallmark cards that say exactly what I want to hear from him. He isn't a letter writer, but he does leave post-its for me on mirrors, the stairs and kitchen cabinets. For our anniversary I compose a love letter recapping each year. He saves all my cards and letters.

Beautiful personalized stationery, particularly the correspondence note cards, are a staple in my desk. A friend once told me that I can fit more on a postcard than most people do in a letter.

I have experimented with fountain pens, elegant ones not the functional kind we were required to use in elementary school where we practiced the Palmer Method of good penmanship. One of the exercises was making circular patterns across the page; keeping the base of our hands on the desk. This is something you can't do with a ballpoint.

Sealing waxes were a passing phase, but I do choose commemorative stamps, like accessories, with care. Katherine Hepburn and Elvis have graced my envelopes along with Archie and Veronica.

The modern forms of communication are great. However, they can't replace that feeling of opening your mailbox and in the middle of bills, junk mail and circulars finding an envelope hand addressed to you. You smile because you recognize the handwriting; you know it's from another endangered species.

Technology can't replace the intimacy of snail mail. Someone's fingers have held the pen, touched the paper, perhaps licked the envelope. My mother wasn't a letter writer, but I have kept lists I found in her cookbooks just to have a visceral part of her. The size and slant of her letters, the generous spacing of her words, the light pressure of her pen are uniquely hers.

I framed my father's last letter, penned the year he died.

"My Darling Girls,
I thought of you every night how nice it is to be loved &
pampered –to be hugged and considered first. How lucky can

you be —five beautiful girls? Can't love them any more than I do.

I love you. I love you. Dad 99% back to normal."

❖❖❖❖❖

At the end of my loop I am back at Ponquogue Beach. By the water's edge I plant my feet and let myself get sucked into the sand, mesmerized by each passing wave. One folds over the other like the flaps on an envelope.

Old School

Snowy plover flight school is being held at the parking lot of Ponquogue Beach. The tiny birds, chattering enthusiastically, look like oversized butterflies fluttering their wings, flying just inches above the ground. Last year I observed them in a more advanced stage when they were starting to fly in formation. I took note of a few slow students and definitely an unruly one.

Looking back over my years as a middle school teacher, other than one or two exceptional students, the ones I remember best were the "bad kids." Since I taught remedial reading as well as English, I generally had the difficult students.

I got my feet wet teaching English in 1967, the year I got married and graduated from college. By the end of the school year, I was pregnant. Actually it was one of my students who announced it. An eighth grade boy I stood in front of every day with his eyes at belly level announced,"Mrs. Helm, you're pregnant." I stayed home with my two children until they were both in school.

I taught reading as a Title I teacher for three years in Hampton Bays, New York, a beach town I call home. In 1979 I got a tenure track job at North Country Road Middle School in suburban Miller Place, across the street from a duck pond. NCR was my home away from home for twenty- two years.

After being retired now for fifteen years, it seems like my quarter of a century career disappeared like the red fox I saw yesterday, but there are still enough tracks and traces to know I was there. I ran with a great pack of teachers, and for the most part I enjoyed teaching because I liked the kids--well not all of them.

I didn't like seventh graders. They had no clue. As six graders, the babies in the building not yet disoriented by hormones, they were little sponges used to group work and a certain amount of coddling. Left on their own the following year, their parents were dismayed when the first report cards hit the mailboxes and there were C's where there used to be B's.

They just floundered on all levels while their voices betrayed them, bumps and hair popped out of their bodies, parts bled, others swelled before they emerged from their cocoons. In addition they had to come to grips with the person who was taking over their body and leaving the little kid they were behind.

I loved my eighth graders who got my humor and allowed me to feel comfortable enough to do goofy things like break into song. For instance, if someone said "help" I belted out a poor rendition of the Beatles' hit. As they entered my room during the holidays or other stressful times, they were greeted with Windham Hill instrumental music, which they initially disliked and later requested.

I introduced the yoga technique of alternate nostril breathing to practice before tests; we played Simon Says when they were distracted and did jumping jacks when we were tired.

I touched kids. Back in my early days of teaching in the late 60s and 70s, it was common for parents to say, "If he gives you any trouble, smack him." I never did hit a student, but I was physical with an occasional ear pull or twist of hair at the nape of the neck, but more often with a hand on the shoulder, a ruffle at the top of the head.

I knew not to touch certain students, the ones who flinched when I came too close or those who made it clear they weren't comfortable. On the final day in June, if it had been a good year, I stood at my classroom door and hugged the students or shook their hands as they left the empty classroom stripped of the evidence of the nine months our relationships incubated.

I closed my classroom door and did whatever I needed to get the job done. One of my colleagues said that I walked the line between mothering and flirting with my pubescent audience. One class surfaces from others. It was a first period reading group of all boys and a sweet conscientious girl. They were tough when they weren't half asleep.

I believed in Behavior Modification, aka bribery. If they received enough points for good behavior and work, they could participate in our Friday breakfast party. It was very popular, and the boys were stricter about the rules than I was. "Don't let Evan have that bagel; he didn't get the points." I served frosty lemonade and pretzels on the beasty days at the end of the school year when we looked longingly out the window at the freedom that was around the corner.

I talked to my students. Once I asked them what they were most afraid of. Two of them answered they knew they were going to be bad. One of them said he wished his parents would send him to military school. I can't tell you what happened to them, but I think their instincts were right. One beautiful 8th grade girl confided that the teachers and parents had no idea what their kids were doing and according to her they were doing a lot.

I gave advice. Since my students were witnesses to me losing both my parents, I told them regularly to go home, thank their parents and tell them they love them. I counseled my girls to be nice to their 8th grade male classmates because they will look a lot different in twelfth grade when they are the top dogs

I defended my students. When other teachers referred to them as dirt bags, I took offense. My reading students for the most part were not college bound; their talents lay elsewhere in areas not valued by traditional education. I tried to be a soft spot in their day by treating them like the good citizens and parents the majority would become.

One such boy, who knew I liked birds and was fascinated by their nests, gave me two he had found during the course of the year. I was impressed with his knowledge of the natural world. The larger nest still sits in my dining room on a shelf next to a stack of books on birds, which I shared with him.

It was especially rewarding when students returned to visit. My favorite memory was a young man who went into the Army where he had found the discipline he needed. He stood before me proud with erect posture and a chiseled jaw line. When the girls came back in bunches they were often unrecognizable, transformed from little girls to glamorous women. I remember one who I didn't recognize because anorexia had claimed her.

I helped them become readers. I had been a reluctant reader. Ironic, I know. In high school, except for *Gone with the Wind* and *Rebecca,* I depended on Reader's Digest condensed books or a friend's summary for book reports. As an English major, I was overwhelmed by the reading and prayed that the writing would get me through, but I think this difficulty helped me to relate to my students.

I chose books that I felt they could relate to and established abandonment policies that gave them permission to move on to another book that might hook them. We made lists of future reading titles, so they could move quickly on to the next book. I whet their appetites by reading the first page of novels or particularly funny or violent excerpts.

The hardest part for me and for many of them was sitting down and getting started, which is why Sustained Silent Reading was so important. Nothing pleased me more than raising my eyes from my book and scanning their faces, some with lips mouthing the words. I noted their physical absorption, their relaxed posture, the lowered blood pressure.

I said bad words, not often but it happened. One sunny day in January when the snowdrops were in bloom on the south side of the barn across from school, a blonde woman peaked into my room, "Hi, Mrs. H. Remember me?"

It took a minute and then her eighth grade face came back to me. "Marjorie." She was home on college break and decided to say hello. Before she left I told her that I was haunted by something I had said to her.

"What was it?"

"I asked you why you always had to act like such an asshole."

She laughed and said she had no memory of it. "I probably deserved it."

I let my students say inappropriate words. When we read Robert Lipsyte's *One Fat Summer,* a book I believed was banned at one time, I assigned roles, and we read it like a play. This allowed them to say things like, "Your ass is grass and I am the lawn mower." Students would ask, "Can I say this word Mrs. Helm?'

"It's not like you are saying it; you're just reading what's in print." It gave them legitimate venues for acting out.

There was a time when I could claim that none of my students left junior high without having read a book thanks to S. E. Hinton's *The Outsiders,* about a group of boys from the wrong side of the tracks who because of no parental supervision skipped school, drank, and got into fights. It was narrated by Ponyboy, a reader, who quoted Robert Frost, "nothing gold can stay." My kids loved the role-playing. I was passionate about the directing, which carried over to my English classes when we read *Twelve Angry Men* and *A Midsummer Night's Dream.* It was magic when a quiet student would become a star.

The year I tackled portfolios for the first time was challenging. Instead of a final exam, the students chose and evaluated pieces of work that demonstrated the progress they made throughout the year. Their folders were bound into portfolios. A group of my favorite students stayed after school, fueled with pizza and sodas, and helped me pull off this Herculean task. The following year students assembled and designed their own portfolios. As a teacher I was always learning.

That was also the year of my divorce when I wore two different shoes to school, not once but twice, and I don't mean two different black shoes but a black and a brown one. Our five day field trips to Washington DC, our nation's capital, sealed the bond with my eighth graders, some of whom had never been out of state.

I was fortunate to have Jim Mahoney as the chairman of our English Department. He was an early champion of Nancie Atwell's workshop approach to teaching reading and writing; I was his disciple. I credit him for guiding me to become the reader and writer I am and to understand that a teacher must be a student as well.

I was guilty of enjoying the sexual taunting of our male faculty. If there had been a sexual harassment suit in my building, the women would have been the offenders. When two of our young male teachers were going to be observed, one was told to do a lot of board work to display his good ass, and the other was better off using an over- head projector to show off his handsome face.

Standing in the cafeteria on lunch duty with the smell of hot dogs past their prime and pizza wafting in the air, I once asked an unmarried math teacher how it felt to know that one particular table of eight grade boys probably saw more action than he did. In our faculty room ensconced in the only upholstered chair, an older red-headed science teacher was the sole male in a prep period with all women. Some of our conversations made me cringe with embarrassment for him. Head bent, legs crossed, he graded papers and barely acknowledged our presence, as his ears turned red.

I got in trouble. During a four day trip to Frost Valley, I fraternized with a parent, a single dad. Slipping two cans of beer in my pockets, we met at the lake one night and got caught. It wasn't so much the clandestine meeting, but that a parent would know that the teachers had alcohol on the trip. Here I was in my forties with all these young teachers, and I was the one banned from the trip the following year.

I have regrets. I failed with certain kids because I just didn't have the temperament or means to deal with them in more effective ways. When a student reaches junior high and still can't read, it's more than an educational problem. I tested and diagnosed students. If there was enough discrepancy between their IQ and their performance, they would be labeled as special-ed students. This diagnosis had distinct advantages, but back then some considered it more of a stigma. Toward the end of my career, I was told to slow down. Too many kids were being classified.

I was sand in our principal, Harry Faulkner's underwear (his words) the years I was a union rep. He hired a handful of obedient, compliant women who turned radical when they hit forty. We had our disagreements on testing and evaluating students. He was a former math teacher who worked with numbers; words were my world. He was left-brained; I was right. But in the end we appreciated and respected one another. At my retirement party he toasted me, "She was grace under fire."

I was happy to be in the trenches. Although I believe a good administrator is a teacher's best asset, I never aspired to become one. The job is too lonely. Times have changed in education, but the things I loved most about teaching, the students and fellow teachers, are still the meat and potatoes of the job.

At times, work was my salvation. During difficult days it allowed me to take a mental break from my daughter's illness, my son's operations, my parents' deaths, and my divorce. It gave me a focus and purpose. The people I worked with were important witnesses to major events in my life. When I retired we celebrated. They were there to toast me at my wedding that September.

❖❖❖❖❖

Now as a retiree my first period begins with a walk across the Ponquogue Bridge, a soaring concrete span that connects our town to the barrier beach and the Atlantic Ocean beyond. I notice how different the bay is on one side than the other. The water on the west is turbulent with white caps, like eels wrestling going in all directions, but once it passes under the bridge, the fight is over. A foamy residue lingers into deeper waters.

The Brick Path

The bridge sits between two different skyscapes this morning. To the east a sapphire blue river chases white drifts. To the west cumulus clusters lined with charcoal choke out the sun looking for a peephole. It's hard to believe it's the same sky.

"I'm not going. You can't make me." My oldest grandchild's words shot into my head and through my heart. Riley Patrick at eleven is like the prickly pear cactus that grows to the left of the bridge: its yellow flower is gone; all that remains is tough and prickly. A far cry from when he used to race into our house yelling, "Mim. Mim." How many times did he tell his parents he wanted to live with Poppa Terry and Mim? Our overt love affair is over.

During the summers I babysit for Riley and Bo, his seven-year-old brother with freckles sprinkled across his nose. They arrive by 7:30 sunburned, with sleep still in their eyes. It's a long day. Both buzz-cut brothers attend the town's summer recreation program from 9-12 in August, which gives their days' structure and me a break.

Up until this year Riley enjoyed our time together. We took road trips on rainy days to IMAX theaters and museums. With my Volvo station wagon loaded with nets, string and chicken legs for bait, as well as a cooler with sliced watermelon and a jug of lemonade, we wiled away afternoons crabbing at Mecox Bay. We picked peaches and picnicked on the North Fork. At home we played cards, scrabble, and board games. He regularly bankrupted me in Monopoly. I told him he could invite a friend to swim in our pool or to play at our beach, but he never did. This year everything I want to do is dumb.

On our last day before school started, I decided to take the boys to the ocean, just a mile away. Something I was reluctant to do. Riley is as heavy as I am, and feather weight Bo is fearless. I lived at the beach when my own children were their ages, but the fear factor as a grandmother is magnified. Bo, the every-ready rabbit, was raring to go, but Riley refused. The line was drawn in the sand. "You can't make me."

I ignored him for the rest of the morning. He knew I was mad. Bo and I went to the beach and left Riley to be absorbed by the couch as he robotically played games on his phone. When we returned wet and sandy, Riley hugged me, "Sorry Mim."

"For what honey?"

"For yelling at you."

"Thanks Riley. I appreciate that. You know that I love you very much, but you better practice riding your bike because I'm not going to babysit for you next summer. You'll be on your own. I'm five minutes and a text away if you really need me."

I ranted on. "I cannot stand to watch you vegetate all day attached to your phone or playing killing games on TV with internet "friends." You're not interested in anything Bo and I want to do, and you make it miserable for us if you tag along."

He nodded speechless.

I repeated the same conversation to my daughter. She protested, "Mom, he'll get worse."

"That's not my problem, honey. You have more recourses than I do. I don't want to be the one taking things away from him. I want to be a grandmother who gives him things."

Last week Riley called me, "Mim, I need some money. Do you think you might have a job for me and Ryan?"

"Sure, Riley. I'll think of something. What do you have in mind?"

"Maybe $20 an hour."

I laughed. "Riley, I pay the man who works for me $15 an hour."

"That would be good."

"Wait a minute. Let me put this in perspective for you. He's a man. He has his own truck and equipment." I knew that if I paid Riley by the hour, it would cost me a fortune, and the job wouldn't be finished. "I'm thinking of a flat rate for the job."

"What do you want us to do?"

"The front walkway needs to be replaced before winter. Maybe you and your friend could take up the old bricks."

In the end, the boys worked for three hours--that included their extended lunch break for man-sized cheeseburgers and a swim in the pool. I also provided work gloves and Gatorade. During one of several rest periods, Riley showed Ryan the banquette where we keep all our games and art supplies. He also asked his friend if he'd like to come to Mim's to swim in the pool next summer.

At three in the afternoon their mothers started to call. The job wasn't finished, but they had worked harder and longer than I had expected. I gave them each $25. Not a bargain, but having Riley with me and happy was priceless.

❖❖❖❖❖

On the road to the old bridge, I am surrounded by a swarm of chirping birds flying so low I can see their white bellies. I am surprised they don't bump into me. Their shadows produce a fast-paced video game. I am with them, but not part of them.

In the parking lot I approach an elderly couple. The woman's binoculars hang heavy on her bony chest. "Excuse me. Are you a birder?"

"Yes. I am," she responded with a German accent.

"Can you identify the small birds that swoop by the thousands like a net being cast into the sea?"

In a clipped speech pattern she said, "They are tree swallows." Then she added, "This is their time."

I have to appreciate that my time with Riley and the five younger grandchildren will inevitably change, but it comforts me to know that the yellow flower is still inside the spiny exterior and will bloom again.

One-eyed Jack

June 20, 2010 Jack

It's hard to believe a year has passed, and it's time again to get a resident beach sticker for my car. Eight of them decorate my rear window.

As I walk the lower half of the bridge, diamonds of sunlight burst as they hit the bay. Like someone madly flicking the on-off switch. Kind of like memories. I stop to retie my shoelaces. As I look down there is a single lens and a few yards farther the broken black rimmed glasses.

One-eyed Jack, my former husband, is in town. If I say my first husband, it suggests the beginning of a series, something I wish to avoid. I am happily remarried. Former sounds more respectful than ex. Since I asked for a divorce after twenty- five years, I feel it's the least I can do.

Jack is up from Florida where he lives in the same complex as his girlfriend. They found each other before I met my husband Terry. It was important to me that Jack be happy and settled. He is a good man.

His visit centers around Father's Day. Jack stays at our son Ashley's summer house, which is down the street from the house Jack and I built in 1976. I still live there. Our divorce settlement was simple. Like filleting a fish, once the bones were removed there were two equal halves. It wasn't contentious because he didn't want me to touch his pension; I wanted the house.

Heading home on the bridge, I look up and notice stoic seagulls sitting like finials on the lampposts as Jack passes me in our son's silver jeep Wrangler. I wonder if he had seen me or not. Jack has a glass eye. He lost his eye in a hit-and-run car accident during his junior year at Villanova University where he had a football scholarship. Sitting shotgun before seat belts were mandatory, he was thrown through the window and suffered a fractured skull. He required extensive facial surgery. Another woman nursed him through the stitches, but I lived with the scars.

The tide is low, creating pools and exposing chartreuse-colored seaweed like tossed tissues. I cry on the way home. The separation of family is still a struggle for me. Initially Jack flew north for Christmas and came to our Christmas Eve festivities, but when the stepchildren started to have babies, my family expanded, and his presence shrunk and disappeared.

June 21, 2010 Noah's Ark

After two cups of coffee, my eyelids are still at half-mast. It's a struggle this morning. I push myself out the door, and my body's internal GPS heads me to the bridge. The breeze is from the south, so this hot day will be fanned by ocean air.

When I reach the bridge, I park my car up by the pavilion. Turning around I watch couples of all sizes and ages moving up the bridge like the ramp to Noah's Ark. A young couple walk with their arms around each other not wanting an inch between them; feeding on the closeness of first love, holding on tightly because it probably won't be the last. But the memories of that love, its discovery and getting lost in it, those memories will be a yardstick by which others are measured; few will measure up because there is only one first.

Further up on the bridge a thirty-something couple power walk. The woman, her fists pumping like pistons, is obviously in the lead, more motivated, driven, making the man look inadequate. I wonder if she is the ambitious one boxed in by her marriage. With no room to grow, she needs to run or fade away.

A third couple joins the parade. They are close to retirement age, bodies filled out imperfectly. The woman I imagine carries more weight than she ever did. The man, in shorts with muscled legs, favors one side, but they walk in unison, an easy gait made for conversation. There is space between them for the woman's animated hand gestures and for the man to swing his arms. At the top of the bridge, they stop and admire the view. He drapes his arm across her shoulder.

These couples remind me of Margaret Mead's philosophy that a woman needs three husbands: one for youthful sex, the next for security to raise children and the third for companionship in old age. I didn't marry my first love, Jack and I had two terrific children, and I feel fortunate to have a second husband with whom I hope to grow old. I'd like to extend this scenario to a fourth couple. We are elderly, walking the bridge slowly hand-in-hand, afraid that it might be our last time because we know these walks won't last.

At the end of the bridge, blue chicory sprouts in between cracks in the pavement. The embankment that spills down into the bay is tangled with bittersweet vines. Stands of Queen Anne's lace, banks of ragweed and other relatives spread out and pop up in between. They are all rooted in sand and don't require care; they just need to be in the right place.

Driving in my direction is Jack in our son Ashley's Jeep. I bend a little to see if it is really him, and we wave to each other.

June 22, 2010 Starfish

I hate to leave my sleeping husband; I'm an hour behind my usual schedule. Sliding out of bed, I open the top drawer in my closet to grab walking clothes.

So easy. Shades of Catholic school uniforms. At the public school I worked at for close to thirty years, my friends and I joked about designing a work uniform. It would be a one piece zip up the front jumpsuit like mechanics wear. We would choose a seasonless fabric and have our names embroidered on the pockets. Borrowing from the military, we liked the idea of stripes for years served and pins for special recognition. Uniforms are comforting timesavers.

Before leaving the house, I *hide* three Father's Day cards in the usual places: a funny one on the stairs, a sweet Hallmark card beside the crystal sugar bowl, and a sexy one on the seat of his wingback chair. Terry started the tradition of three cards for special occasions the first year we met. Anxious to get back for our Sunday morning ritual of reading the *New York Times*, eating a big breakfast while watching a string of news shows, I pick up the pace.

Coming up the other side of the bridge is a man with an orange baseball cap. I realize it's my former husband Jack. He looks thinner than I expected. He is a big man, a disciplined athlete. His orange cap and shirt, University of Miami colors, is the giveaway. Jack, a Florida resident, is still an ardent fan, more so than our son who graduated in 1993.

We greet each other with a brief hug and kiss on the cheek. I change directions and walk with him. "How are you, Jack?"

"I'm feeling good."

"The back's okay?"

"No more pain."

"Haven't Riley and Bo grown?"

"Riley's gonna be a *big* boy."

"They eat so much crap."

"She better watch him. He's got the Helm gene."

"Doesn't Melissa look great?"

'Yeah, she does."

"Have you and Ashley played golf yet?"

"Tomorrow."

"Do you think he and his live in will get married?"

"I don't think it will happen."

He talks about the weather, one of his favorite subjects, asks about my sisters, gives an update on his brother and sister. Jack and his friend Judy are going on another extended extravagant cruise. This time to the Baltics. I walk him back to our son's Jeep and say good-bye.

"Stay well. Be happy." I reach up, and he hugs me.

As I head home across the bridge, the sun has burned off the fog. It saddens me to see a dead starfish staining the concrete. They have great regenerative powers; it was just in the wrong place.

I feel lucky that Jack and I have created new lives and loves. I pick up the starfish. Its pebbled skin is hard. It's dead, but I throw it back into the bay anyhow and watch it break the reflective surface.

Home

Instead of maintaining my usual brisk pace on the Ponquogue Bridge, I stopped in the middle and paid homage to a perfect Saturday morning. It was June, summer's waiting room.

I heard the click of a gear, and a shirtless cyclist appeared in front of me. He opened his arms as if to embrace the day, "My God look at this." He turned to me, "Gorgeous isn't it?" As he started down the bridge, he exclaimed, "It's like a slice of Ireland here in Hampton Bays."

I wanted to yell after him, "Where exactly?" but it didn't matter. I just loved the idea.

My parents, three and four generations removed from their ancestral homes, never celebrated being Irish. There was no corned beef and cabbage, no talk of the old sod or its politics or relatives living there. But for most of my life people have told me how Irish I look. I have always been drawn to the literature, the humor, the brogue and especially the men. I feel Irish.

Although I have traveled through Europe and lived in Norway, I had never visited Ireland, mainly because its cuisine seemed to be limited to hearty breakfasts and Guinness--until the rise of Darina Allen. A proponent of the slow food movement and considered the Julia Child of Ireland, she began its gastronomic renaissance. Ireland was featured as a foodie destination in The New York Times Travel Section in 2005. When my husband, Terence Patrick Meehan, asked what I wanted for my 60th birthday, I told him that I needed to go to Ireland to connect with my roots.

A year later at Shannon airport I was sure I saw my cousin Francis in a business suit sprinting through the terminal. And I was reminded of a conversation with my old friend who said she couldn't get over how familiar the faces in Ireland looked--to see yourself and your relatives in a foreign place that feels like home.

We spent the first night of our sixteen-day trip at Longueville House, a Georgian Country Home, on a 500 acre estate in the heart of the Black Water Valley. We were revived from our flight by tea and scones served with the richest butter, mounds of clotted cream and homemade strawberry and black currant jams. Trout and salmon fishing as well as seasonal hunting could be arranged, but we were content to borrow Wellies and walk the walled gardens, orchards and fields.

After a superb dinner served by a young French waiter, we retired to the living room where we sank into down filled cushions on a sofa in front of a crackling fire, sipped coffee and nibbled sweets.

In the predawn pale I looked out from our bedroom window at a frosted still life of sheep on the front acres rimmed with ancient trees. In the distance lay the Battle of Cornwall formations. I imagined my family owning this property before it was seized by the English and later reclaiming it..

Our next stop was Shanagarry and the Ballymaloe House, which except for its windows and a bright blue door was wrapped in wisteria. Ballymaloe House and Cookery School are run by the Darina Allen family.

Terry and I paid $50 apiece to audit a cooking class where as guests we were invited to the head of the line of future chefs to sample the day's lessons. Since we live by the beach at home we were intrigued by the delicious gelatin dessert made from seaweed. Before we left, we toured their glorious vegetable garden and its centerpiece, a shell cottage with an interior inched with a mosaic of shells.

Continuing south to Kenmare, we stopped at Cobh where we encountered a small group lingering after a first Holy Communion at Saint Colman's Cathedral high on the hill. Although poverty wasn't apparent, I couldn't help but think of Frank McCourt's *Angela's Ashes* when we saw the veiled little girl in a long white dress, cape and matching umbrella. Her male counterpart wore a pin striped suit with satin vest and cravat. Cobh was the last port of call for the Titanic and also where many emigrants left for America. Were my people starving or looking for adventure or following a loved one when they came to America?

Sallyport B&B in Kenmare, winner of the Tidy Town Award, was home for three nights. It's ideally situated to explore the Ring of Kerry and the Beara Peninsula. Our innkeeper, Jane, looked so familiar I asked if we had ever met. She didn't think so, but she had lived and worked in the States for many years. She embodied Irish hospitality as she bustled about serving breakfast selections with ease in her comfortable home filled with antiques and Waterford vases arranged with flowering branches from her garden.

We visited the Derreen Gardens at the beginning of the Beara Peninsula. The Rhododendrons, considered an invasive plant, in shades from yellow to purple were massive. A rich patina of moss, lichen and ferns upholstered rocks and roots and snaked around trees and across branches similar to the bewitching garden at the Blarney Castle where I meditated while my quiet husband kissed the Blarney Stone. Perhaps I am a reincarnated Druid.

Although I felt at home in Ireland, the driving was definitely foreign. It was disconcerting to stare at the driver's seat in an oncoming car, and find no one there. In addition, the roads, particularly on the Beara Peninsula, are so narrow that at one point the road we thought we were on turned out to be a driveway to a Buddhist Retreat Center.

Curves and switchbacks make navigating even more difficult. If we began to recognize sheep, I knew we were lost. At one point we passed a roadside shrine whose inscription read, "O Mary Help Me," and I completed the invocation with to find our inn. Even on the other side of the Atlantic, Terry refused to ask for directions.

Driving on Dingle Peninsula was like driving through Boston during 'the big dig' where we could see where we wanted to go, but we couldn't get there. All the signs were in Gaelic, which added to our confusion.

Our destination, Gorman's Clifftop House, is the sort of place I would have been happy to curl up on a couch in a nook painted persimmon and read for three days. I sat for an hour and watched a midnight blue sky weigh down on electric yellow embers until they were crushed into molten gold spilling into the bruised and purple sea. Whoever said Ireland is all about green has never seen a sunset in Dingle.

At dinner we talked to Sile Gorman, a dead ringer for Rita at my gym at home, about how Irish kids used to come to Montauk and the Hamptons to work for the summer. I recalled an experience in Montauk where my son had given me a Day of Relaxation at a famous spa. When I had free time between scheduled appointments, I wandered down to the beach. A blonde babe, a black Adonis and an Irish lad manned the concession. They told me that for a nominal fee they would provide me with a beach towel, chair and umbrella. I was astounded that the small fortune my son paid for the day did not include a place to sit or shelter from the sun. On principle I declined their offer and said the sand would be fine. In minutes the Irishman was beside me dropping fluffy towels on a nearby lounge and adjusting the umbrella for me. He simply said, "My Mum would have done the same."

As we were leaving, Sile had just gotten back from a tip to Limerick She was walking towards the Inn with TJMax bags hanging like weights from both hands.

We hoped to catch some music in Doolin, a surfer town, but our timing was off. Instead we watched boys in wetsuits paddle quite a distance to Crab Island to catch the waves. Ponquogue Beach, K Row and the Bowl are meccas for surfers in our town. The local dudes would be impressed with the amount of work required of their Irish counterparts before they even reach the swells.

That night we went into town to a local pub for dinner where Patricia Connery, my Aunt Dorothy's doppelganger, played an instrument that looked like a portable vacuum cleaner. Her songs led me to believe that she was unlucky in love. In her sweet reed thin voice she told of a long-suffering woman who had brutally killed her husband, while the women in the audience nodded knowingly as they sang along with the tra la la refrain.

In Bally Vaughan, Terry found the 13th century tower Yeats and his wife used as a summer home. It was surrounded by fields of cow parsley and marjoram in dappled sunlight. His other home was in Sligo, where according to a cousin my family can be traced. I'd like to think Yeats and I are related.

In the morning we hiked in Connemara National Park where any plant above six feet tall is wind pruned. On our way down the trail, I had to stop a curly headed blonde and ask if his name was Brophy because he looked so much like a family friend.

Our sixteen-day trip took us as far west as Westport. The west coast just feels different from the south. The south is like a married love, strong and easy and the west a passionate lost love. We never made it to the north, the land of "the troubles," where both our families can be traced. I have envisioned myself wearing a cape and riding boots, romantically linked to a freedom fighter and ready to die for the man or the cause.

In Malcolm Gladwell's *Outliers*, he mentioned Scotch-Irish as ferocious cultures, and although he didn't suggest that we are prisoners of our ethnic histories, he stated, "Cultural legacies are powerful forces." This makes sense to me. When I am at a parade, I place my hand over my heart when our national anthem is played, but when the bagpipers pass that hand turns into a fist.

Our final destination was the Dromoland Castle, now a luxury hotel that is conveniently located to Shannon Airport. The castle has everything. What interested me was trap shooting. I had never held a gun, but with the assist of a wiry gentleman and his tobacco-stained fingers, I outshot my husband. But the recoil hurt my shoulder, so I gave him the rest of my round to practice. I used my injury as an excuse to drain the crystal decanter of Irish Mist, cognac with a taste of honey, found in every room.

Since we got lost often during our visit, I surmised that the reason there are so many B&Bs in Ireland is because travelers decide they just can't drive anymore and knock on someone's door and ask for lodging. My husband said that it's because once you are absorbed by the Emerald Isle's beauty you can't bear to leave.

Generally, my favorite part of a vacation is coming home, but I cried on the way to the Shannon Airport the next morning. It wasn't that I didn't want to go home; it was like I was leaving home.

❖❖❖❖❖

Back in Hampton Bays, my eyes sweep across the vista from the Ponquogue Bridge. The barrier beach with its grass skirt pocketed with goldenrod lies between the crystal bay and the silver sea, which makes me think of the many times we took a wrong turn in Ireland and discovered little harbors, rocky inlets and magnificent beaches like ours.

Complete

The day before we left for Mexico to escape winter, I walked the Ponquogue Bridge. The sky was holding on to the snow as long as it could before it let go. The gentleness of the falling flakes contrasted with the geometric ice floes in the bay that jockeyed for positions with the current. One seemed feminine, the other masculine. Made me think of men and women.

I love men, more specifically I am drawn to Irishmen, who have poetic hearts but souls that are sometimes sucked into the black holes excavated by their alcoholic fathers. Brooding silence that can last for days is more comfortable for them than words. This has been my experience. Maybe this lack of talking is simply a male trait, not just particular to the Irish.

An Irish woman, I am a fighter who needs to blow off steam. I want to have it out and be done with it. Kiss and make up. It has taken me a while to understand a man's need for time alone and that I can cope with stretches of silence with the help of my female friends.

During our morning coffee hour, my husband Terry handed me *Newsday's* cartoon section, "Check out *Pickles*. It's good."

Two old guys sitting in rockers are reading the newspaper. One says to the other, "Scientists have discovered that women have a 'language protein', which may explain why women are so chatty. That's why the American gal says about 20,000 words a day while the typical guy only says about 7,000." His friend asks if there is a cure. The other responds, "We can only hope."

Sometimes when I am talking, my husband will throw his head back, roll his eyes and fake snoring. He likes quiet; I need to talk. After my forever friend Ann's husband died more than twenty-five years ago, I called her every day. When I got divorced, she checked on me. We never run out of things to say. Thank God for girlfriends.

❖❖❖❖❖

My husband and I spent the month of February in Mexico. Terry's daughter, Beth, and her family were with us for the first week. We were recovering from a low point in our marriage involving a lack of communication concerning money, but the presence of our grandson Jayden and the warmth of the Mexican sun melted the ice between us.

On Valentine's Day I began to work on my annual present, a list of 50 reasons why I love him. There are the standard ones: you make me laugh; you have a truck; you are my private dancer. It's definitely easier and more interesting to jot down the endearing things as they happen throughout the year: such as your phone screen is a picture of me on the Maid of the Mist at Niagara Falls; you agreed to a large party on 12/12/12, when more than six for you is a crowd; you packed my pillow in your suitcase. It's tough to create the list in one day.

So on February 14th I was lost in thought about love while wandering down lushly landscaped paths lined with towering Pharaoh's Fans, Elephant Ears, and Lion's Claw. Instead of focusing on my husband, I found myself thinking how much I treasure my female friends who like rainwater fill my upturned leaves. My friendships with them enable me to love my husband as deeply as I do. Once I toasted a newly married couple and told them that the best gift they can give each other is to be the best person you can be, for that I need my husband *and* my women friends.

I have always been surrounded by Eves. I grew up with four sisters, attended an all-girls high school and a women's college. Besides my sisters and dear friends I consider my "pall bearers," I am blessed with many circles of friends who share similar interests, including bridge and golf. The members of my book clubs and my writing groups, especially The Windmill Writers, nudge me to expand my literary horizons to become the serious English major I didn't bother to be in college.

Since I retired I have come to appreciate older Queen Bees. My first writing circle was with Taproot, a workshop for women over 55. I had just reached that age, the location and time were ideal, but why would I want to hang around a bunch of old ladies? Then Helen Fitzgerald walked into the church social room in a black leather jacket. She flipped her steel grey hair from her face and read jaw-dropping poetry.

The Full Circle, a cooperative farm on North Mecox Road in Southampton, is where I met earth- mothers Sandy and Dorothy. Ageless Sandy, sporting a tiny ponytail, is the boss. I call her Mother Superior.

At the farm I am comfortable playing the drama queen, an unfamiliar role. When Sandy asks, "How's the family?" I regurgitate any obsessive thoughts I have been harboring. "Oh my god Sandy, my daughter is getting divorced. Where will she live? Maybe with me, but for how long?" "Should I refinance and extend my mortgage or try to pay it off?" "Look at this thing on my face. Do you think it's cancer?"

She shakes her head and loops her arm through mine. "You have a lot on your plate. Children are always a worry. Things work out. Come. Look. We'll be eating asparagus soon." And Sandy's right. I see their green heads pushing through the winter blanket.

In conversation about yoga with Dorothy, who bends her body in half when she weeds and walks with the grace of a former dancer I say, "I really should..."

Before I can start my litany she squeezes my hand, "Eliminate the word should from your vocabulary." I am happy just kneeling next to Dorothy, slipping single seeds into the earth.

❖ ❖ ❖ ❖ ❖

With a moon hung like a Mexican hammock in a black sky, Terry and I celebrated Valentine's Day. Our cards were mirror images of each other. He always gives me three. In one he wrote, "A successful marriage requires falling in love many times, always with the same person."

Besides enriching my life, my female friends bridge those times before my husband and I fall in love with each other again.

The Scent of Another Woman

The fog is rolling in. At the bridge the visibility is zero. I feel like I am walking through a tunnel of grey cotton candy. I can't quite make out what is in front of me. My nose wrinkles. I whiff the perfume of a woman gripping tiny weights before she appears through the misty drapes.

Even though I don't have a good sense of smell, I am sensitive to certain odors. I gag walking down an aisle of scented candles. The pine-tree-shaped air deodorizes hanging from a driver's rear view mirror leaves me oxygen deprived. Those room fresheners that plug into the wall are worse than the malodorous smell they are trying to disguise. Enclosed in a car with a group of perfumed women, I run the risk of being knocked unconscious.

However there are natural smells I love: freshly mowed lawn, salt air, sheets dried on a backyard clothes- line. At Christmas I hang an evergreen wreath with a red velvet ribbon above our bed. Two little balsam wreaths halo the single beds in the guest room, which is always so cold on the north side of the house that the freshness of the greens hits you when you open the door.

In May small square vases filled with lily of the valley sit on our bathroom vanities singing spring. Lilacs bloom outside our bedroom window. I love the fragrance of hyacinths—white, blue and perky pink. I keep a stem or two in my office for aroma therapy.

Culinary scents whet my appetite. The zest of lemons, limes, and oranges wakes up my sinuses. The savour of a garlicky scampi, rosemaried potatoes, thyme- marinated chicken creates a delicious anticipation. And what's a morning without the aroma of brewing coffee?

Some memories are stored in the olfactory center. In the back of my guest closet on the right hand side is my mother's tiny yellowed mink jacket with her name embroidered in the satin lining. It's been there for eleven years. I probably could have had it dyed or reconditioned or made into a vest, but I was afraid that if I did, it wouldn't smell like Mom anymore. Arpege was her perfume. I want my children to have a piece of my clothing that they can bury their faces in, inhale deeply and remember me. The problem is I can't find a perfume I like.

My first one was Prince Matchabelli's Wind Song followed by Nina Ricci's L'Air du Temps. I dabbled with a Ralph Lauren rose fragrance and then switched to Laura Ashley #1, a light scent I wore for years until they discontinued it. Since then, I have gone au natural, but lately I feel the need for a signature fragrance. My oldest friend has always worn Chanel #5 that smells right on her, but not on me.

Until I find the right perfume or possibly invest in a custom fragrance, I have borrowed the scent of another woman. At the annual summer bazaar at Saint John's Church in Southampton, I found a turquoise and pink shawl draped over an antique chair. It wasn't in the warrens filled with clothes and accessories where it belonged. Maybe someone decided not to buy it and left it the room with fine furniture.

It's a work of art. The center is turquoise framed by an intricate pink paisley pattern outlined in the corners by tiny iridescent blue, pink and orange sequins. Larger marine blue and copper spangles are surrounded by dusty pink French knots.

It smells like another woman, I thought when I first pressed the fine wool fabric to my face. I breathed in a deep rich intimate memory of a mysterious woman with gypsy blood. Someone who is confident to stand out in a crowd. Someone whose presence lingers long after she is gone. Someone who has loved deeply, traveled extensively.

I was that woman when my husband and I spent a month in Mexico last winter. I wore it every night. When I stood up to leave an outdoor restaurant one evening with the shawl grazing my shoulders, I glanced back at the chair. Three pink sequins sparkled on the seat.

On the way to our suite, my husband and I brushed by leaves the size of elephant ears along the jungle path lined with purple and silver stripped Wandering Jews, canopied by palm fronds. The clouds were moving so quickly that it made the full moon look as if it was racing through the sky before it dropped into the darkness. After lovemaking that night, my husband asleep on his side, I noticed a single orange sequin on the whitest part of his body.

A Million Bucks

The sign with upside down letters hangs like an alien landmark on the corner of Shinnecock Road and Foster Avenue; I know something's up. When I reach the top of the Ponquogue Bridge, I can see a helicopter on the right side of the parking lot and a tented area on the left. At the bottom of the bridge, a guy is stopping traffic. I'm the last one over the bridge before the copter with the film crew lifts off like a giant dragonfly. I sprint over to the beach pavilion where a crowd has gathered. "What's going on?"

"They're filming a New York State lottery commercial. See that sports car by the tent? Some guy's gonna drive it across the bridge."

"How cool." I am surprised that this scenic vista isn't used more often in advertisements and movies.

Three months later my husband calls me. "Hey Dee, check this out." Pointing to the TV screen he asks, "Isn't that the Ponquogue Bridge?"

"Yeah, that must be the commercial I saw them filming. Cruising in a Jaguar XKE across our Bridge a regular looking guy, somewhere on the other side of forty with a sense of wind in his cropped hair, muses the question, "What would you do if you didn't have to worry about money?" The camera scans the pewter bay and the ocean, a silver plate lit with golden rays.

Since I rarely buy lottery tickets, the chance of me becoming an instant millionaire seems slim, but the good news is as grand as it would be I don't need a cashier's check with a series of zeros to feel like a million bucks.

Throughout my life I have felt rich because of my ability to enjoy other's good fortune. The next best thing to driving a platinum 350Z or flying your own Beechcraft twin engine or owning a house with the best view in the Hamptons is to have friends or relatives who do. Rich by association.

This feeling extends beyond possessions. Because Irene Tully is on a committee of every museum on the East End I feel more cultured. Knowing Irene's husband Bill, a lobster fisherman, gave me more cred as a local when I was a suburban transplant. Attending Almonds off-season Artists and Writers Dinners makes me feel hip. Interesting by association. Vicarious pleasure is my winning ticket, but that doesn't mean I don't enjoy the real thing.

Visiting with Irene recently, I mentioned that I had perused Isa's Consignment Shop in Hampton Bays for the first time and was impressed at the quality of the merchandise: Searle coats, designer dresses, high end bags and shoes. I confessed that I was lusting after a Hermes scarf that lured me to the back of the tightly packed shop where it hung with a few others on hooks behind the owner's desk. Even from a distance their colorful designs called to me; I sensed Hermes. To me a Hermes scarf is more than a cut of silk. It's classic elegance with an air of Grace Kelly, Audrey Hepburn, Jackie Kennedy, idols of my youth.

I admitted that I have always wanted one but could never justify the price for an accessory, $250 even for a second-hand one. Shoes, pocketbooks or jewelry yes, but a 35-inch square of material, no. But as each birthday nears I think, this will be the year I'll treat myself.

Irene, who appreciates my love of finer things, chirped, "I have one. It's been a decorative piece in my drawer for years. I never wear it; you can have it." The gift had outlived its signature orange box with brown trim, but I was giddy with delight.

The next day she delivered the silken treasure, appropriately called Les Clefs or The Keys, designed in 1965 with a royal blue border and 47 golden keys. When I wore it for the first time with jeans, a crisp white shirt and a blue cashmere cardigan, two friends commented on how great I looked. I have arrived. I now own an iconic fashion statement.

At our annual Labor Day champagne breakfast at the beach I posed the question, "What makes you feel like a million dollars?" I instructed my friends sitting in a semi-circle in our chairs, the ones that are low to the ground, to think outside of the family and the things we know that really matter. I was pushing for something material like my scarf, but except for flying in first class, they listed simple things that make them feel happy: eating ice cream from the container, slipping into a bed crisp with ironed sheets, coming home from anywhere, having a good hair day when it counts, laughing until you're doubled over.

However, I am not alone in thinking that a piece of clothing can make one feel rich. On my return lap on the bridge yesterday I walked with Barbara, a woman who lives down the road. She asked when I was going to have another yard sale since she loved the things she bought at my last one, especially a black fox headband. She told me that she wore it to work during this winter's polar vortex and her co-workers wanted to know if she had won the lottery. "No." she said, but she felt like a million bucks.

Summer Nest

The bay is striped this morning with dark and light blues like a summer tablecloth. When I walk farther up on the Ponquogue Bridge, I'm glad to see the ospreys are rebuilding their nest. Last week it was just a vacant platform, one of Super Storm Sandy's casualties. I too have to feather a new roost, since we have rented ours for July and August.

It's not the first time. After I was divorced, I leased my house for several summer seasons. Since I live in the Hamptons, New York City's summer playground, rentals are in demand and the money is substantial.

Since Terry and I married in 2001, we have only let someone "borrow" our house two weeks at a time while we were on vacation. Because we knew the people, we just pushed our clothes to one side of the closet and made a little space in the drawers. But longer rentals entail a lot more work. The good thing is it forces us to clean out and organize every room, every closet, and every drawer.

Friends of ours who live in Southampton Village have been moving out of their home every summer for years. They treat it as a business. We've adopted that approach. This is our job, which will provide the extra income we need. It's something Terry and I will work on together.

Fortunately, I had taken pictures of our pool and garden at the end of last summer that enabled me to post our property in January as a "Hampton Classic with pool and garden oasis" on Vacation Rental by Owner.

We made a master list and broke it down into weekly schedules. Besides the usual seasonal jobs, we are taking care of maintenance issues like rusting heating vents, inadequate shelving in closets, and painting, which have been easy to put off. I tape and sand; Terry wields the brush and roller. After the steps in the foyer shined with a fresh coat of paint, the front door looked shabby. Of course one thing leads to another. It's a huge undertaking.

So our tenants can claim the house as their own, we remove personal articles like photographs. The hard part for me is what to throw away, what to give away, what to pack, what to store, and what to leave. Moving is easier.

When I complain to friends how exhausting this is they say, "Well, you've done it before." Yes, when the house and I were thirteen years younger.

Thirteen years ago I had a handyman I could boss around. He came when I called, did what I asked, when I asked and even put up with my occasional breakdowns. Dealing with my husband, who I wouldn't trade for the world, is stressful at times. Talking to Terry about home projects is kind of like praying. I know God hears me, but we're not on the same timeline. He is a slow and meticulous worker. I assure him that his very good is my perfect. I don't want him to die or quit on me. So instead of yelling, "Why the hell are you building a potting bench on the side of the shower house instead of power washing it?" I hold back, and trust.

How could I not have noticed how mildewed and ripped the outdoor cushions were? Why didn't I replace them last year? Why didn't I have the sectional cleaned years ago instead of flipping cushions? If only Terry hadn't waited until the last week to hang the new door that has been resting against a wall for months. What have we been doing?

Two weeks before we had to hand over the keys to strangers, our house started to act up very badly, like a child when she realizes that her parents are going out and leaving her. The pool water hadn't cleared yet, spraying hadn't deterred a resident ant colony and our refrigerator died. I found myself practicing alternate nostril breathing, a yoga technique, to force down the sense of panic rising from the pit of my stomach. "It's all going to work out. Somehow the minor miracle will happen." I try to reassure my husband as well as myself while we're standing in the family room surrounded by clear storage containers and the damp cushions from the just cleaned sectional.

I had forgotten how old some of our appliances are. When the stackable washing machine that had performed perfectly for ten years began to make torturous noises, our service man declared it not worth fixing. One of the problems was finding a unit that could fit into the space. Plus it had to be delivered in five days, which left us with three choices. $2,000 later we have a set that seems to have half the capacity of the former one and dances around the laundry room if an extra towel is added.

It's ironic that preparing our house for the rental that will provide us with money is costing us a fortune. We remind ourselves we are not changing the fixtures on the track lighting, replacing the pool pump, and installing air conditioning for renters but for ourselves. When we reclaim our house in September, we will appreciate all our work. And hopefully next summer we will be better prepared and realize a profit.

We rented our neighbor's apartment above his garage. It's clean, whitewashed and airy. The saving graces are an outdoor shower, storage space in the garage and room on the ground floor, which I anticipate will become my office during the day and Terry's cave at night.

In addition to preparing our house for others, I jot down articles I want to take with us for comfort and a feel of home. The list is longer than my grandchildren's Christmas list. I whittle it down: our down pillows, monogrammed towels, the blue cashmere throw, our coffee mugs and a few favorite framed photos

If we survive this move, I will be pretending that we are on vacation despite the fact that there is no dishwasher, and I will be doing laundry at my kids' houses. Will I miss our pool that I rarely use? Friends have offered a lounge at theirs. Nobody is expecting us to entertain.

Maybe I'll spend more time at the ocean which is still just a mile away. Maybe this is the time to buy loose tea and brew our own. Maybe I'll make the time to read the pile of books I carried with me and stacked on the shelf that runs under the windows in the living room of our aerie.

Thirteen years ago when I rented my house I felt unmoored, adrift. My single status allowed for a gypsy lifestyle, but now I am at home in my marriage. Terry and I have worked together as a team over the last couple of months. I think this bird house is going to be our love nest.

On my return walk, I notice that the land seems to have reclaimed the bay. Only rivulets and small puddles remain by the north side of the bridge. Before I know it we will be returning home. But in the meantime, like the osprey flying with strands of grass, I'll add finishing touches to my summer nest. I'll buy a dozen of votives at the Dollar Store to light up windowsills like fireflies.

Span 25

Spin

Needed to check out the surf this afternoon, inhale some salt air and be calmed by the constancy of the waves rolling in and out like inhaling and exhaling. The parking lot at Ponquogue Beach is empty except for the driver of a muscle car doing doughnuts, spinning out of control across the asphalt pavement. I was spinning today too.

Took my first spin class this morning. My friend Ann had a mastectomy two weeks ago, and I am her driver, committed to doing whatever she wants. Exercise has always been higher on her list than mine. Since winter is not a walker friendly season and she didn't want to join the local gym, we signed up at Southampton Recreation Center to use the indoor track, a second floor balcony. We walk the track, walk and talk. I do most of the talking then I say, "Your turn." And I practice listening.

Since February is heart month they are running specials including free spin classes, so instead of walking today we sign up for spin. Ann, of course, has done this before and even has the special shoes that clip into the shoe slots. We take bikes in the back row and are surrounded by mainly twenty-year olds and two middle-aged men.

The female instructor, Susie, gives me a few rudimentary instructions: the height of the bike seat should be at mid-hip level, the lower red knob adjusts the tension, harder to the right. The screen, which I cannot read without my glasses, registers your miles and calories burned. She says go at your own pace. The hardest thing is getting used to the saddle: a six-inch unpadded, stationary, hard plastic triangle. She's not kidding.

The music starts with songs not in my repertoire, but it's not as deafening as I expected. I am still able to hear Susie yell, "Pick it up." Sweat breaks out. I shed the vest, then the turtleneck. The room is dark. I am glad that the disco light on the ceiling isn't turned on. Has anyone ever fallen off one of these things?

"Okay, sprint." My competitive spirit clicks into gear, and I cycle as fast as I can. Next we are supposed to stand up. When I attempt it, I slam my right knee into the water bottle holder. Then I hear, "Saddle," which means we sit down again. I decide that I really don't need to stand, but after a while my ass is so sore I do, just to give my rear end a break, and I smash my right knee again. I swear I can feel it swelling. I wonder if when I get off this thing, it will it be like stepping off a bar stool and realizing you have no legs.

Every now and then I glance at Ann hoping she will talk or raise her eyebrows, but she is focused. The chemically straightened hair that frames her face is damp and wanting to curl. She looks tired to me. Where does she get her energy? I wonder if she has a mantra in her head "Fuck this cancer. Beat it. Beat it."

I don't think about how long we have been friends, how she called me to come to the hospital twenty-five years ago when her husband died at 42, how I picked out his clothes for the funeral parlor. I don't think about how I know she will tell me what to do when I can't figure something out, how she listens to my daily babbles. I don't think how she is so damn smart and as a lawyer reads the small print on everything. I don't think how I could imagine life without her. I think my ass is burning, and I will never fuck again."

"Saddle. Now just push with your right leg." I'm back. I have to concentrate on this simple exercise. "Now the left." I look at the clock--9:40. Thank God, maybe it's a 45 min. class. No, she probably would have started some cool down by now. Please God maybe a 50 minute. "Dig a little deeper." One humming bird of girl is spinning so fast her legs start to blur, or am I blanking out. "Water break." Hurrah. My water bottle is empty. My hair is slipping out of my ponytail.

Ann is going to lose her hair, which is so thick it takes an hour to dry. She was tortured with the decision to have chemo or not. "What did Amanda say?"

"Do it, Mom." Amanda is a dentist like her father and her grandfather. Is her opinion medical or daughter based? Ann's numbers are in the gray zone, where the decision is more patient driven than doctor directed. She hates the idea of putting poison into her body.

I tell her. "You're doing the right thing. Keep networking with other women and talking to different doctors. Eventually you will hear what you need to hear. Then you will make the decision, and it will be the right one."

This morning she told me, "I am going to do it. Have chemo." She had spoken to a cousin, an oncologist nurse; she said do it. "I'm going to lose my hair."

"Oh God this makes it real. I am so sad for you, Ann." We held each other and cried. Her hairdresser said to come in before she starts chemo and he'll cut her hair, and when it's time he'll shave her head.

I spin faster, "Fuck this cancer. Fuck. Fuck it. Fuck it."

"Stand up and climb the last big hill in front of us. Work it. Work it. You're doing great. We'll be on the down side soon." The cool down finally starts at 9:50 and I am grateful that it's almost over. It's just beginning for Ann.

Perks

From the top of the bridge, Oakland's Restaurant and the commercial fishing boats are in sharp focus. The bay is clear as a river bed, yet I can't see the time on my watch. My distance vision is good but, as a recent trip to the city reminded me, I am blind without my reading glasses.

Unaccustomed to taking the train into the city by myself, I passed the exit for the Long Island Railroad Station at Ronkonkoma. Realizing my mistake, I zipped off the expressway into a gas station to reconfirm directions.

When I got to the parking lot, I didn't have time to cruise the free parking areas. Of course, the only spots left in the garage were on the top level, and paranoia set in. First, I couldn't park on the outer row because if I hit the gas pedal too hard, my Volvo station wagon would fly off the roof as in an action-packed cop movie. But that would probably be preferable to the other fate.

But that would probably be preferable to the other fate: returning late at night, walking alone, I'd hear another set of footfalls. Or I would open my car door, slide in and before I'd have a chance to swing my left leg into the car, a hand would reach out from under the chassis and grab me. In both scenarios, I am raped and killed. I chose the center aisle spot under a floodlight.

Running down the three flights of cement steps, across the street to the waiting train, I jumped on without a ticket. The tall dark-haired conductor moved down through the car calling, "Tickets. Tickets." I thought his night job might be a vendor at Madison Square Garden, "Beer here. Beer here." I told him that I knew the tickets were more expensive when you buy them on the train and asked if it was cheaper to purchase just a one-way. He said it didn't matter, so I paid $19 for an off-peak one-way ticket to Penn Station.

The woman seated next to me leaned over and asked, "Are you a senior citizen?"

Dressed in a pale lavender Calvin Klein suit, Pucci design fitted blouse, and Chanel flats, I thought I looked like a stylish middle-aged woman, not a senior citizen.

"Why?"

"They can't charge you extra to buy tickets on the train if you are."

"Really? What do they consider a senior citizen?"

"62."

"Really. Excuse me conductor." When he came to my side, I flipped out my license and told him that I was a senior citizen and according to this woman, I should pay less.

"Yes, that's correct. I didn't think to ask you."

"Thanks."

"You'll save enough money for a drink at lunch."

"Sounds good to me."

"That's $9.00. Here's $10 change."

"There are perks to being a senior."

I thanked my seatmate and rummaged through my pocketbook for glasses to read the newspaper. No luck. This meant that I was practically blind. The commuter towns whizzed by in a blur.

The plan was to call my friend when I arrived at Penn Station where she would be waiting. Together we'd walk down to Bryant Park Grille to meet another college friend for lunch.

Disembarking from the train, I realized that I couldn't make the call because I couldn't read my phone book or the numbers on my phone. I figured I'd have to find a store to purchase the glasses. Then I spotted a small information desk in the waiting room manned by a kid in a uniform.

"Excuse me young man, I wonder if you can help me."

"What can I do for you?"

"My friend is somewhere in the station waiting for me to call, but I left my glasses at home, and I can't see. Could you please look in my phone book under B and find her number? Barbi, Mary Jo--on the left-hand side towards the bottom." I realized I sounded just like my mother.

"673- 987 -3345" he recited.

"I'm sorry." I laughed, "I can't see the numbers. Holding the phone out to him, "Could you please dial it for me?" He rolled his eyes and complied. Maybe he was thinking of his mother? Grandmother?

Mary Jo was waiting at the top of the escalator. We linked arms as we emerged from the bowels of Penn Station. On the sidewalk I felt as if I had been blindfolded and spun around. My friend pointed us in the right direction. Our first stop was to buy glasses. It was comforting to be with friends who knew me when the only glasses we talked about held a drink.

Not a Drop to Drink

The vista from the top of the Ponquogue Bridge never ceases to amaze me as it changes from season to season, day to day, hour to hour, minute to minute, but what doesn't change is that it features Shinnecock Bay, with Tiana Bay under its arm like a little brother, both lorded over by the mighty Atlantic.

"Water water everywhere but not a drop to drink." As of today, March 23, 2015, I haven't had a drop of alcohol since December 1st.

Well, that's not true. Christmas Eve I sipped a festive Tito vodka and cranberry juice with a big squeeze of lime. For a family dinner in January, it seemed a shame to enjoy a perfectly grilled beef filet without a glass or two of a Grapes of Roth Merlot.

When my cousin Barbara stayed with me for a few days in March, I would have been a poor hostess if I didn't toast her birthday with a flute of prosecco, and had another to remember her husband Billy who died on Saint Patrick's Day last year, and then raise a glass to Mari, her 97-year- old mother, whose funeral we had attended earlier in the day. But other than those occasions and a few others, I have abstained from the spirits for three months and 23 days, but who's counting?

I love my earthly pleasures. I have always said that I would eat and drink whatever I wanted until a doctor told me not to. It wasn't a doctor's order but a pain that prompted my decision. With a few carefully planned experiments, I realized that if I didn't drink I didn't have the jabbing pain under the left side of my rib cage or the discomfort in my chest that felt like a heart attack. I was hoping abstinence would be a temporary solution.

My doctor suspected gallstones or a gallbladder problem. "How much do you drink, Denise?"

"Well, I am not satisfied with just one glass of wine."

"How often?"

"Most every night."

"Two glasses of wine for a woman is the equivalent to four glasses for a man."

The sonogram was negative for a gallbladder problem. Next stop was an appointment and tests with a gastroenterologist. At the intake I was given a prescription for a proton acid blocker, an appointment for an esophagogastroduodenoscopy which would film one end of my alimentary canal to the other, and a recommended diet for GERD, an acronym for gastro esophageal reflux disease. No coffee, no alcohol, no chocolates, no tomatoes, no citrus. Life isn't worth living. There is no way I could give up all of my favorites. I had to make a decision. Caffeine or alcohol?

I decided that at times I can't function *with* alcohol, but I can't function *without* caffeine. I'm not a shot- between-the-toes type of addict, but I need my daily fix of coffee.

In the morning I stumble out of bed and crawl up the stairs where the Folgers is already brewed waiting for me. I heat the skim milk in a stainless pitcher while I go to the bathroom. Then I pour the liquid drug into my white mug with the pale blue interior, stained at the level where the coffee stops, before I add the steamy milk. As I sit on the couch with my legs stretched out in front of me and take the first sips that will transform me into my public self, I think I have made the correct choice.

Then 5 o'clock rolls around and whistles blow, alarms ring, sirens wail. It's cocktail time. Except for me.

What a letdown. Boring. Dinner, which used to be my favorite meal, becomes a glorified lunch. In the past we didn't just eat; we dined. I prepared artfully plated delicious food accompanied by a glass of wine.

Besides the standard gallon bottle of pinot grigio, I like to support and sample local wines such as Shinn Estate's Sauvignon Blanc and Bridge Lane White Merlot from Lieb Cellars. In the summer Wolffer's Rose is my pink lemonade.

People tell me I am a good cook; I explain that I am really just an Ina Garten technician. But without the company of wine, I became disinterested, even in just thumbing through her tempting cookbooks. Who cares? My husband, who doesn't drink, could eat cereal for dinner. Cheerios were starting to look good to me. But I pushed myself. "How about a sandwich tonight?"

The results of my tests were mild gastritis, esophagitis Grade A (the least) and a sliding Hiatal hernia. The doctor told me to continue the medication for a total of 8 weeks and then wean myself off. Eat small portions often, and yes, I can drink but not on an empty stomach.

Since I had broken the nightly habit and found that I could enjoy dinner reasonably well without a bottle of red or a bottle of white, I decided to wait for a social opportunity to uncork my alcoholic thirst. If my husband drank, it would have been much harder for me to give it up.

At the next party I accepted a glass of white wine as I would a chalice. It always felt good to have a stemmed glass in my hand. But to my dismay as it kissed my lips and touched my tongue, it tasted sour.

As my sister once said when I told her I really didn't care for chardonnay, "The second glass is always better." This time I didn't go back for seconds. At book group, where my friends' blood type is PG (pinot gringo), I poured my old standby. This one also struck an acidic note. What has happened? Have I lost my palate for wine? Is it possible I don't like to drink anymore?

❖❖❖❖❖

Drinking and I have a long history. On the mornings after my mother's Card Club meetings, my sister and I would troll the kitchen and the dining room table--covered with dirty dishes, glasses and crumpled napkins--looking for leftover dessert. I loved my mother's signature grasshopper pie loaded with crème de menthe set in a dark chocolate crumb crust.

Sometimes if there was a maraschino cherry, an orange slice or a wedge of pineapple in a glass, we'd sample unfinished drinks that stood next to the ashtrays overflowing with lipstick stained cigarette butts.

Amid the chaos of family gatherings, my mother's father, Par, ensconced in a wing chair with a cigar and martini, would squeeze my hand with a vise grip and ask, "What's new?" I'd shrug my shoulders and he'd respond, "New York, New Jersey." Then he'd give me the olives in his martini and return to his newspaper. Rolling it around my mouth, I'd extract the burn of the alcohol before I bit into the briny morsel.

I didn't take a shine to beer as quickly as the subtle taste of vodka, but somewhere between my first brew at age 11 and my favorite bar stool at The Straw Hat in Mineola, it became a staple.

Drinking liquor was like smoking, an acquired taste. Who really loved that first drag that resulted in a coughing fit and left you a little lightheaded? Maybe it was the light- headedness that made me stick with it and practice those deep inhales.

Or was it the desire to seem grown up? The only adults I remember who didn't smoke were my two grandmothers.

Or was it the fact that my boyfriend smoked and what was sexier than him leaning in with a lit match cupped in his hand to light my fire?

It seemed a natural progression. We just graduated from cokes at the candy store to beers at a bar by 1963 when we were seniors in high school. There were few rules and none of them had anything to do with drinking and driving. We drank Budweiser from the bottle. No canned beer or glasses. We all had phony proof. Even though I was very young looking, I never had a problem because my high school boyfriend had a five o'clock shadow

It was a party every weekend with lots of dancing. Drinking made me a much better dancer and less concerned if I was a sweaty mess by the end of the night. At The Coach House, a great make-out place that served pitchers of whiskey sours to couples in booths and played Johnny Mathias, we'd grind the night away on the small dance floor.

Instead of hanging out in bars in Philadelphia where I went to college, there were frat and house parties, since the drinking age was 21 and harder to fake.

At the end of my junior year I turned twenty and was engaged to my first husband, a former Villanova football player who was four years older than I. Elaborate tailgating and post game parties with Bloody Marys and champagne at stately homes that rimmed the campus filled my date book. He belonged to a country club where they were too polite to ask for proof. I felt terribly grown up. Cocktails with royal names like Brandy Alexander, White Russian, and after dinner favorites, Remy Martin and Stingers, were in vogue.

Three years later I realized that I wasn't ready to be grown up, but by then I had a daughter and a son. My daughter was a joy. I was fascinated by her, content to just watch her sleep.

When my son was born seventeen months later, the dynamics changed. Everything was multiplied and I was divided. Sophistication took a back seat. So did drinking and smoking. As a mother I felt I needed to act more responsibly. It took me nine months to give up the nicotine habit. I missed it most when I was drinking, but that was less and less.

As soon as my children were in school I went back to work because we had been told by the Women's Lib Movement that we could have it all--only our husbands hadn't been informed. So we did it alone.

During my life as a harried working mother, my drinking was mainly restricted to weekends, which meant many lost Sundays nursing legendary hangovers. Those toe curling headaches and time spent in the cold tiled bathroom hugging the toilet probably helped to curb my intake. I drank to the tune of "Is that all there is?"

Some people don't like the sense of losing control when they drink. I drank for that very purpose. When I tossed back a shot of tequila instead of the usual sensation of liquid flowing down into my stomach, it shot straight into my brain. I wanted to feel that heady looseness and freedom. I wasn't happy in my marriage and alcohol was a way to escape and numb those thoughts I couldn't deal with.

When I was 40, my daughter left for college, followed by her brother two years later. My nest was empty. That time gave me a chance to reassess my life and admit that my children were the glue of my marriage. Of course, at that my point in my life I didn't appreciate that they would both be back, in and out for years.

After my divorce, drinking became a toast to life not a way to drown in it. I don't think I started to drink regularly until after I retired, when I didn't have to worry about the next day. It became a habit, part of the unwinding of the day, a partner to good food, a friend. Occasionally I would stop just to make sure I could. There's enough addiction on both sides of my family to be wary. As my wise friend Alice always says, "If you treated alcohol moderately in your younger years, it can be a friend in old age."

My plan is that when I start to drink again I will imbibe less and more mindfully. So I have decided that I can live without the company of a night cap, but when I go out to dinner I will order a martini with three olives. I can eat the olives first, so I won't be drinking on an empty stomach.

Rising Star

My daughter Melissa's few possessions sit in my foyer outside her childhood bedroom where she used to sneak out the west facing window when she was a teenager. Large plastic bins are stacked in the corner surrounded by smaller colored containers like gifts under a Christmas tree carefully labeled in her artistic script: board games and art supplies, wine glasses, frames and photos. A stuffed animal lounges on top, and a basketball is wedged in between. The arms of a large blue tin star poke out from behind the pile. It used to hang over the bed she shared with her husband.

Boxes and shopping bags stuffed with books fill the back of my Volvo station wagon. I just don't have the energy to move them into the house. After 14 years and two sons, she's done. There is no turning back. The decision is right and brave, but life after is scary.

She confided, "Mom, I feel like I'm you."

And I wanted to scream, "But I had a career and well-to-do parents who financially padded the way for me. You and your brother were in your early twenties." But the times and her situation are different.

This divorce feels like a splinter in my mind. I need to walk and clear my head. Lost in thought, I am surprised to find myself on the bridge. I try to suck in the peace. It's dead low tide. The sand mirrors the bay's pattern, a furrowed brow. Further out, seaweed like mermaid's tresses dances with the tide. I think I need to go with the flow, relax, trust that things will work out the way they are supposed to. I know that's what my daughter wants from me. I know it's what I wanted from my mother. I needed her to just say, "Everything will be fine. You are going to be fine." over and over again.

Melissa and her husband are going to a mediator because they can't afford a lawyer. It seems to be working well. The woman serves as an impartial moderator who allows each party to be heard. They have decided on alternating custody. The boys will spend one week with their dad, and the next with their mom, which means with us since Melissa has moved back home. The house that she hoped to rent fell through the day before she was supposed to move in. It was a big disappointment.

Last week was our first week all together and it was fun. Bo, a second grader with an old soul, who told his mother that he's "not mad, just sad," organized a family game night. We laughed through *Family Feud*. We planned healthy meals the boys would eat: tacos, roast chicken, spaghetti. Pre-teen Riley likes to cook with me. Melissa has gone out of her way to maintain the organized chaos.

This morning the brilliant sun catches the glass dome over one of the goose-necked streetlights turning it into a crystal ball. I wish I could see into the future. I gaze up and ask: will my daughter find a good paying job? Will she fall in love again and be lucky like me? Will the boys be okay? Will she find a place to live before summer rentals dominate?

Looking into the bay I realize that what looks like a bed of black kelp is actually a flock of Greater Scaups. They seem to be in flight school. One group at a time takes off and flies a short distance to tiny Sedge Island. As the group gets smaller and smaller, I focus in on one bird that keeps flapping her wings and going no place. Finally she takes off.

I used to tell Melissa she was an untapped keg of dynamite. Now I see her shedding unhappy pounds, morphing back into the girl in a favorite photo taken when she was ten. She's wearing a navy blue dress and pin-studded beanie, smiling broadly with her arms crossed as if to say, "Bring it on."

Back home I reach behind the packing containers and pull out the blue tin star I bought for Melissa one Christmas. I place it like an ornament standing on top of her boxes.

I think her star is rising.

Thanksgiving

I didn't get up early enough the day after Thanksgiving for the detox class at Good Ground Yoga, instead the couch called to me and I obeyed. Propping my upper body against down-filled cushions and stretching onto the sunlit sofa with coffee and pumpkin pie, I read last week's New York Times. My recovery time after holidays has increased with age. By afternoon I felt the need for crisp air. Since the wild winds of previous days had subsided, it was time to walk the bridge.

At the ocean pavilion I notice the sky is filled with birds. I walk down to investigate. It's common to see a squabble of seagulls tracking a school of bluefish, but this was different. It's as if the stars fell from the sky and turned into seagulls. I thought there might be a large carcass washed ashore to attract this myriad of gulls.

A couple bundled in down jackets, each with binoculars hanging like pendants around their necks, were walking towards me as I made my way down the beach in the grooves created by the fishermen and surfers' four wheel drives.

I greeted the couple, "That's quite a spectacle over there. What's going on?"

"Looks like the recent nor'easter brought acres of skimmer clams to the surface. There are oyster shells too."

"Wow. I've never seen anything like it. A feeding fest."

"It's Thanksgiving for the seagulls."

Our Thanksgiving dinner this year wasn't a feast for the multitudes but a love fest of six. My daughter and son and their wonderful new mates were with us to give thanks. Both my children like their mother have found love later in life.

In the past we celebrated Thanksgiving with my daughter's in-laws. However, she and her husband separated right before Thanksgiving two years ago. They now have joint custody; he has the boys for Thanksgiving. Around the same time my son was in the process of ending, a seven-year relationship with a live-in girlfriend. On that turkey day my kids just felt like hibernating in the home where they grew up.

For the last two years we have tried to stuff their voids with roast turkey, half a dozen sides and their favorite Briermere's blueberry cream and pumpkin pies, The break- ups did bring my children, who are seventeen months apart, closer together, since neither one of them cared much for their sibling's partner.

This year at our table, set with fall finery and glowing candles, I raised my wine glass and began a round of toasts, "I am surrounded by love. Lauren and Dave, I am thrilled that you are with us tonight because you make my children very happy and nothing makes me happier. And to you, my love. Happy Thanksgiving, Terry"

My bachelor son was next. He openly professed his love for Lauren, whom he had met on Match.Com four months earlier. I don't remember the exact words. I just heard I love Lauren, and I was dancing in my seat, calculating that at 38 she was still young enough to start a family.

In the summer, I had casually asked Ashley about his dating experience on Match.Com. He'd given me a quick rundown on the women he'd met. I do remember him saying that one of them had spent time on Ponquogue Beach because her grandmother had lived in Hampton Bays. That girl was Lauren.

Lauren and Ashley's apartments are at either end of the Brooklyn Bridge, so they bike to see one another daily and spend most of their weekends at Ashley's house here in Hampton Bays. One long weekend they met Lauren's family at their cabin in Pennsylvania to hike and canoe. The progression of each week's activities verified my initial feeling. THIS is IT.

Ashley's declaration "I love Lauren" was still echoing in my head when Lauren and Dave made their toasts. I don't remember the details other than their happiness to be with my son and daughter and to be welcomed by us.

Thirty years ago Dave had Melissa's name tattooed on his chest. He was her high school boyfriend until he left for the Navy. They went separate ways, but the feelings remained. Through Facebook they had reconnected. He was living in Texas and was married with a son. The whole situation seemed a fantasy and I was worried that Melissa, a romantic like her mother, would be crushed in the end.

But Dave, a man who sets goals and makes things happen, loves my daughter. Another thing I love about him is that he tells

Melissa how wonderful she is and says the same things I've been saying for years, only she listens to him. He is now divorced, and his company is moving him to New York in late December.

Although he came for visits during the last two years as often as he could, I think the long distance relationship was good for my daughter, allowing her time to reclaim herself and focus on her sons who are now anxious for Dave to move in.

Moving around the table, Melissa expressed her gratitude and appreciation to Terry, Ashley and me for the help we have given her during the past two years. When Ashley moved to a new building in the city, he gave the entire contents of his place, from silverware to flat screen TV, to his sister to furnish her small apartment.

She was promoted to a new position at work and Terry and I filled in when needed with the boys. It's easy to help Melissa because she works hard and plus she is always generous with "Thank Yous."

When it was Terry's turn he thanked Melissa for roasting a turkey and Dave for frying one. Ashley, who Melissa and Dave call 'the chosen one,' questioned whether Melissa was trying to rack up points for the favorite child position. Some things never change.

After dinner and the dishes, we played word games and looked through two boxes of old photos. Lauren wanted to see pictures of Ashley when he was a child. She cooed, "You were so cute. Look at how long and blond your hair was." While Dave laughed, "I remember this one from prom night."

At ten o' clock before I said goodnight, I watched the four of them laughing, having fun together. I went to bed emotionally sated.

Years ago when I was divorced and single, Melissa gave me a copy of *Simple Abundance,* a daily meditation book. The author, Sarah Breathnach, extolls the power of keeping a gratitude journal. I purchased an animal-print bound book with a gold cord place marker and began the practice of listing five things I am grateful for at the end of each day.

Once I got started, the possibilities seemed limitless, but when the fall harvest of my love life was paltry and I was facing the prospect of another long cold winter alone, it was more challenging. I came up with things like a toilet plunger, aspirin, clean underwear, coins to roll and Kleenex.

Then I met Terry who magnifies the happiness in my life. This Thanksgiving my blessings are like the seagulls, sun flashing beneath their wings, too numerous to count.

Solo

There's a lot of bird activity around the Ponquogue Bridge this mercifully mild March morning. Swallows sit like clothespins on the telephone lines. Walking up the first stretch of the bridge, scanning the flat bay, I spot a sole swan. I wonder where her mate is. It's surprising how many of my friends have become widows. I call their sorority the Swan Club, one group I am not anxious to join.

I was without my mate on a trip I recently took to Florida. My husband Terry and I usually travel together, but he had already missed four weeks of work while we were on our February vacation, so I went by myself. The plan was to visit two sets of friends, who were both spending the winter in Venice, Florida, and then on to Orlando where my sister Suzan and her husband, Jim, live. I would be gone for a week.

Besides being a career woman for decades, I lived alone for seven years after I got divorced. I don't want to be one of those women who can't function without her man. Still, in the ten years I have been married to Terry I can see how much I rely on him. If it has a motor, he takes care of it. If it requires a remote or a mouse, he is the problem solver. I thought we shared the stress of traveling but after this adventure, I realized how much I depend on him.

After I checked in at MacArthur Airport, I thought I listened to the agent when she told me the gate number: A7. I arrived in plenty of time, had breakfast and got comfortable with my book, sitting with my back to the gate. At one point I did stand up and ask a woman in a line which flight she was waiting for, just to make sure it wasn't mine. Shortly after I heard the loudspeaker clearly announce, "Denise Meehan please report to the Southwest ticket counter." I jumped up, identified myself and was told that my flight had already boarded at gate A9. I raced over to the waiting attendant and quickly moved to the back of the plane. So much for the early boarding pass I had in my hand. When I landed, I called Terry, "I almost missed the plane…"

At the end of a visit with my friends, they drove me to a Budget Car Rental. Behind the counter a short squat man named

Manny was on the phone talking about the birth of his baby. "Yeah, we were working last night and she went into labor."

He handed me my paperwork and motioned me to an assistant outside who put a fob in my hand, explaining the car had a keyless ignition. Oh, God, modern technology. I had never heard of such a thing. "How do I start it?" Then I noticed the ON push button. "I don't think this is going to work for me."

"Okay, how about this one?"

The grey car looked nice. I slide into the driver's seat to adjust the seat and mirrors and instantly the hairs in my nose began to burn. The car smelled like an ashtray. Not thrilled, I looked around, and there on the backseat was a lemon. Immediately my superstitious mind registered, *this is a sign*. Someone has left a lemon to signal to the next driver, *don't take this car*.

I called my husband, "What should I do?" He told me to ask for another one.

I could hear Manny before I entered the cinder block building. "It's a boy, Sebastian Manuel..." When his conversation ended I told him my problem, including the superstitious part.

"It's just a piece of fruit that probably fell out of someone's shopping bag. Then more agitated he added. "I don't believe in superstition; I only believe in God."

"Yeah, but if there's a piece of fruit rolling around on the back seat, I question how well the car has been cleaned."

"Okay, you want a different car?"

"Yes."

"Do you want a black Mustang?" I couldn't tell if he was being sarcastic, but I pictured myself in the fast lane speeding down Route 4 and spending the night in a Florida jail.

"No. I just don't want a lemon that reeks of cigarette smoke."

"Pick what you want."

Fortunately I remembered that my suitcase was still in the trunk of the first car. I walked back into the lot and decided that the four-door Mazda next to it looked substantial. It smelled fine and looked clean. When I returned to the office Manny gave me the keys. I handed him the lemon.

He asked, "What do you want me to do with this?"

"Make lemonade." I laughed.

He shoved the lemon into his mouth, bite down, juice running through his fingers, and he began to eat it. I figured the guy was running on no sleep. I made a quick exit.

The brakes responded well; the car felt solid, but a whining noise told me that although it seemed to be an automatic, it hadn't shifted gears. Driving for three hours going 80 mph in first gear would not be a good. I shook my head, I can't go back there. Panic was setting in. I pulled into a parking lot and called Terry. I described the console. He suggested pushing the stick shift as far past the drive line as it would go when I felt it was time to shift. That worked.

The monotony of a highway lulled me into a sense of relative calm although the thought of getting lost rolled around my brain like dice. I kept my cell phone on my lap. Country western music was omnipresent on the preset radio stations. I began to think that if a rental car is my biggest problem, I had it easy. Plus I could look forward to my sister chauffeuring me around for the next few days.

After a few days with my sister I headed to the Orlando Airport for my flight home. I was tested again. The car had to be filled before I returned it, but I couldn't open the gas tank. I looked for a lever inside, but it wasn't where I expected to find it. An attendant came over to help me and had to come back again when I had trouble closing the gas cap.

At the airport I doublechecked that I had the right gate and sat facing it.

After I landed and retrieved my luggage, I called Terry. Minutes later I walked outside to find him waiting for me. He folded me into his arms.

The best part of being away is coming home.

❖❖❖❖❖

My walk this morning confirmed that the Atlantic Ocean is still where it was a week ago. Raising my eyes I notice the contrails of a jet, chalk lines on a blue board. Once in a while I think it's a good thing to travel solo to remind myself that I can. So someday if I am like the swan without her mate, my heart may sink, but I'll know I can navigate the waters and stay afloat.

Song and Dance

Even though the fog isn't dense, just a halo along the shore line on this low tide morning, I can hear the bass of a fog horn. The twitter and song of spring arrivals contrast with the hoarse cries of the gulls. Peg Allen and Mary Layton, Mutt and Jeff friends are walking towards me on the Ponquogue Bridge. "Morning girls. I always expect to see you dancing up the hill." Mary, as short as Peg is tall, is a local tap dance instructor.

Because of a friend's insistence, I took Tap Lessons at Adult Ed several years ago. I wasn't really interested, but I had recently seen the Rockettes in their dazzling costumes at Radio City Music Hall. I decided to keep her company. Investing in tap shoes was something I thought could wait, but without the click of the metal tips on the wooden floor, tap lost its appeal.

So those lessons were as short lived as my ballet lessons as a six year old under similar circumstances. I didn't have the ballet slippers for the first class probably because my mother didn't do things in a timely manner. Instead, I wore white cotton anklets and practiced positions on the shiny floor until I fell, landing on my nose which bled profusely. I was too embarrassed to go back.

My father, my first dance partner, taught me how to do the box step. In bare feet I would stand on his shoes with my left arming reaching for his shoulder and my right hand in his as he moved his feet in an invisible square.

He loved to jitterbug. The only moves I found easy were when he'd throw me up on one hip and then the other or slide me through his straddled legs like a rag doll.

Then there was the cha cha. One-two cha cha cha. I finally got the steps down, but they didn't connect with the music especially if turns were involved.

As a preteen in the late 50s after school I watched *American Bandstand*. I held on to the door handle in our den as I tried to imitate the moves of big haired, blonde and beautiful Justine with her picture perfect partner Bobby or their dark counterparts Arlene and Kenny. Arlene's tresses were teased and shellacked into a beehive. Kenny's greased hair was combed high on top and slicked back on the sides to form a seam called a D.A. or duck's ass.

The couples not only were mirror images of each other, they moved as one. My door knob was a perfect partner because I didn't have to follow or know I was out of step.

My high school boyfriend, Sean Gallagher, whose mother was an instructor at Arthur Murray Studio, was a terrific dancer. In the early sixties at the Bayside Yacht Club he taught me something similar to the Lindy called the Savoy which required running leaps on my part to match his 6'4" stride. In the last will and testament of my high school class, I was left a step stool to reach his shoulder when we slow danced. Slow dancing was always my favorite.

When I was in college in Philadelphia, there seemed to be a monthly dance craze: the Mashed Potato, the Monkey, Pony and the Jerk to name a few. These dances didn't require a partner, but by the time I learned the steps, the next fad had started. I was much relieved when the loosey goosey do your own thing came into vogue. It freed me, but I still danced to the lyrics not the beat. Directional problems and lack of coordination weren't my only challenge. I lacked rhythm.

I just don't have an ear for music. In a Linguistics course in college we sat in cubicles in the language lab where we were instructed to raise our hands whenever we heard a new phoneme. I never did. It all sounded the same. When I realized students around me were raising their hands; I mimicked them.

Each of my five grandchildren has said, "Mim, don't sing." when we are in the car, and I join them in the "ABC song" or "The Itsy Bitsy Spider". If asked to name that tune based on an instrumental recording, I would probably guess some Christmas carol since without words that's what most melodies sound like to me. I am tone deaf.

Thanks to the internet, I have just diagnosed myself as beat deaf, a form of congenital amusia which is an inability to feel musical rhythm or move in time with it. I can hear normally with the exception of beat and rhythm in music. This condition affects four percent of the population in Western Europe and North America.

There were two of us at a local concert at the West-hampton Beach Performing Arts Center. I was sitting with my friend in the eighth row of the intimate theater listening to a beyond-old Blues singer. He sat on a stool in the center of the stage sweating as he riffed and picked at his guitar, grunting and groaning while the audience clapped along.

Suddenly he stopped. He stood up, and walked closer to the edge of the stage. Pointing into the dark, he rasped, "White girl. Like this." and he clapped his hands to the internal beat.

At first mortified, I thought he had discovered that I was the one who slapped my hands together a nano second off, but he was directing his comments to a woman in the fourth row. Now, when I clap along in public, I keep my hands low or carefully try to copy someone, like my husband.

My husband gets the beat and his body responds. His deceased wife could dance to anything. I feel bad for him that we are not that dancing duo who takes over the floor. Although I enjoy music and like to dance, he knows I don't experience music like he does. One of the musical things we do share is if one of us says a word that reminds us of a song such as "moon" we might both break into a rendition of "There's a Moon out Tonight" or "Blue Moon".

When we are at home and our wedding song Van Morrison's "Someone Like You" plays on our sound system, we find each other. He puts his arm around my waist and pulls me close. I place my hand on his chest over his heart. We barely move. He sings into my ear. "I've been all around the world marching to the beat of a different drum. I realized the best is yet to come. Someone exactly like you …"

Mama Said

Despite the fact that it feels like summer on this October day, the landscape reveals the truth. Sweet gum trees with star shaped orange to purple leaves, scarlet sugar maples, and golden poplars line the streets in town and flame on neighbors' lawns. By the Ponquogue Bridge bordering the bay, wheat colored grasses, raisin leafed bushes and browned goldenrod announce fall's arrival. Things are changing.

My son, Ashley, was married on September 25, 2014. Almost exactly a year before he had appeared in our foyer at 8:00 one morning, "Mom, I want you to meet Lauren."

They stood in their wetsuits as we chatted. I swear she looked adoringly at him, and he was blushing. After they left, I said to Terry, "She's the one."

I didn't want to gush for fear that a mother's approval could be the kiss of death, but I knew Ash would wonder what I thought of her. So I carefully worded my text. "Lauren is darling, perfect smile, love her positive attitude and that you two paddleboard together. Harvard ice hockey!"

He replied, "She's great."

Weeks before the wedding he texted, "Mom check out YouTube for Lynyrd Skynyrd's 'A Simple Man.' I was thinking about it for the mother-son dance." Sitting at my computer I read the lyrics while I listened to the music. I particularly liked these two stanzas:

"Boy don't you worry, you'll find yourself
Follow your heart and nothing else
And you can do this, Oh baby, if you try
All that I want for you, my son, is to be satisfied."

"I love it, Ash, but can we do the chicken dance to it?"

My phone dinged the arrival of his next text. "Ha. The lyrics are great, but it's that Southern rock. Hard to dance to. I'll see if there are other versions."

I thought it's not as if we'll be doing the foxtrot. I don't think Ashley knows any official dance steps. He prefers to act out the lyrics or fall back on standard moves such as mowing the lawn, the shopping cart or fly fishing.

My reply, "We can just rock back and forth. The words are the important thing to me."

Still today when I see this tall, wonderfully built, handsome man, I am surprised. Where is my skinny little boy with the long blonde hair? I had him for 44 years and God knows, no one is happier about this wedding than I am.

Even though he is a successful Wall Street broker and had his own apartment in the city, in his twenties and thirties he still came home on the weekends to do his dirty laundry. I stopped washing his clothes when he was fourteen, after I unearthed yet another pile of clean folded clothes that was easier for him to throw into the hamper than to move neatly into his dresser drawers.

When my husband Terry and I started dating, Ashley was 31. I decided, for more than a few reasons, that he needed his own place. Besides my desire for privacy, I didn't want him to become the stereotypical Irish bachelor who still lived with his mum. I broached the subject, suggesting that financially, socially and emotionally it was time for him to invest in real estate and have his own home.

"Mom, I don't have time to look at houses."

"Do you want me to find one for you?"

"Yeah, yeah Mom, that's good."

The following weekend I had three listings lined up in Hampton Bays, where he has deep roots. He bought the one I knew he would, which happened to be a mile down the road. Ashley gave me his credit card and carte blanche to furnish and decorate his bachelor pad.

By the time Lauren arrived, it was time to redecorate. Lauren loves a project; I love all the improvements they have made. There is definitely a division of labor. Stopping by with farm eggs and kale from my plot at the school garden, I found Ashley in the kitchen wrapped in an apron baking thumbprint cookies while Lauren was painting the sunroom.

A week before the wedding, I got a text from Ash and Lauren.

"Mom you need to pick a mother- of- the- groom song."

"I thought we had, "A Simple Man"

Lauren responded, "UUGH."

I got my Irish up. This is our song. It's for mother and son to decide and we had. But I took a breath and remembered how nerve-racking it is to be the bride. Ashley loves this woman and I love them together. I don't need to make waves. I also know who would get the life preserver.

"I'll see what I can come up with." I listened to dozens of them as tears rolled down my cheeks. The reality of losing my son hit me; he's not mine anymore.

He texted back, "Tick tock tick tock."

I texted him, "Check your email. Too long for a text."

I wrote, "Ash, listening to all these songs it dawned on me that I have waited your lifetime for you to be happy in love. But I realize it's bittersweet because your deference now will be to your wife, Lauren, as it should be.

"So I appreciate the choice of 'A Simple Man,' but I found a few that are easier to dance to: Carol King's 'Child of Mine,' 'Ordinary Miracle' by Sarah McLaughlin, and Van Morrison's 'Days Like This.' Check them out."

Ashley replied immediately, " *Days Like This* was on my list. Love Van Morrison. I really like Stevie Wonder's *Uptight Everything's Alright,* but I'm afraid that I would start imitating his blind style of dancing. I am sure it would be a real crowd pleaser, but I will refrain."

I was especially glad that Van won out because his *Someone Like You* was the song Terry and I danced to at our wedding. *Days Like This,* a mix of blues and Celtic soul backed with heavy sax, became the official anthem of the peace accord in Northern Ireland. The lyrics include:

When everything falls into place like the flick of a switch...
When all the parts of the puzzle start to look like they fit...
Well my mamma told me there'll be days like this

Whenever I daydreamed about dancing with my son at his wedding, I imagined blubbering through it saturating his shirt with tears, but ours turned into something entirely different.

Lauren and her father stepped off the dance floor after waltzing to *The Way You Look Tonight*. Ash and I held hands and took center stage. I had no idea what to expect but I saw his fun-filled expression and nodded, "I'll follow your lead."

We opened our arms like figure skaters and greeted our family and friends. Then I imitated his hand-over-the- head lasso twirl followed by a spin and we were off. My daughter was hysterical laughing. Her brother at his best. At one point Ashley and I came together in a traditional stance. "Mama said they'll be days like this. I love you, Ash".

"Love you too, Mom."

Jack

The din of a distant motor moves closer as I walk the Ponquogue Bridge this morning. The north wind flaps open the Rosa Rugosa petals like a wide-mouthed scream. It must be eight o'clock because Reveille is pumping from the speakers at the Coast Guard Station. The trumpeting of a new day triggers a reservoir of uncried tears.

My former husband, Jack, has esophageal cancer and I am overwhelmed by the unexpected emotions I feel. I can't talk about it without crying. We have been divorced for twenty years, five shy of the number we were married. He moved to Florida years ago and flies to New York once or twice a year to visit our children and grandchildren. I am always happy to see him, but I don't miss him when he leaves. I rarely think of him, so I am surprised at this flood of feelings.

I look down at the mess fishermen have left on the bridge: coffee cups, soda bottles and plastic bags. Time has sealed the memories of that part of my life, compartmentalized like they never happened. Then I look up and the ocean lies silent in front of me.

❖❖❖❖❖

Jack and I met on a blind date in January of my junior year in college. The joke was he is blind in one eye, the result of a car accident at the end of his third year at Villanova, where he played football and had expected to go pro. A Maryland boy with good manners and the voice of a southern gentleman, his friends called him Wood Eye or Wild Man because of his feats on the football field.

Four years older than I am, he knew what he wanted and wined and dined me in a style to which most college boys couldn't compete. The financial compensation for a fractured skull, facial scars and the loss of his eye afforded him a Shelby Mustang and a British racing green Triumph TR4, membership at Fairmont Country Club and a rich boy lifestyle on a teacher's salary.

When I brought him home for the first time my mother said, "I hope you're not leading this one on Denise." At the end of my third year in college, I returned home to New York for the summer, leaving Jack in Philadelphia.

A few days later he called, "I'm at Marco Jewelers. They have a diamond at a good price. What do you think?"

Standing in my family's blue and white wallpapered breakfast room, I held the wall phone with the ten-foot cord to my chest. I hesitated. We had slept together by then, the nagging virginity gone. I thought we would get married eventually, but not yet. I wasn't ready.

I replied, "I was planning to waitress with my girlfriends at Herb McCarthy's in Southampton for the summer."

"Oh."

When I heard the disappointment and hurt in his voice, I backpedaled, "Sure, okay," I said.

A grey velvet box rests in the back of a bedside drawer with my wedding and engagement rings from my marriage to Jack. The design is delicate and different, not the typical solitaire setting that was popular in the 60s. The platinum wedding band had a series of diamond studded branches that interlocked with the engagement ring. A tip of one end had broken off and never been repaired. Some of the smaller diamonds had fallen out. When I took it off, a 25-year-old groove at the base of my ring finger remained.

Over the years the good times had faded and the disappointments, both his and mine, were left on my tongue either to justify why I left or explain how unfinished I was and that his bear hug had become a cage, not a comfort. But his illness pushed those things out to sea and like the tide rolling in, the sweet memories come back.

With the balance of Jack's insurance settlement we were going to buy a house, which I had little interest in, still focusing on passing final exams and saying good bye to my college life. I wasn't ready to settle down. Jack suggested a grand tour instead. When I asked my mother what she thought, she didn't hesitate, "You'll eventually have a home, but you won't have this opportunity again." Jack and I honeymooned for two weeks in the Bahamas and then flew to Europe where we spent four weeks in four countries.

Highlights gather in my mind, like the day we spent with the hotel bartender and his pregnant wife at a bull-fight. It featured world renowned matador El Cordobes. In the walled city of Avilla we sat in the sunny section of the Plaza de Toros and shared wine in goatskin sacks. Winding our way back through ancient roads, passing men on donkeys, we took turns singing. Ramon and his wife, who didn't speak English, serenaded us with Flamenco songs; we countered with Beatles' tunes and "God Bless America."

Spain was followed by England. The cool greenness of London was a relief after the heat of Madrid. It felt like home, being able to converse in English in the pubs, until the surprise of the closing bell rang at 11p.m.

I remember the robin's egg blue two-piece velour outfit I bought in Vienna after we had stopped for chocolate torts in the Black Forest. It was my Christmas outfit for years.

I loved our time in Paris. Our hotel room had floor to ceiling French doors that opened onto a tiny balcony. I have a picture of Jack in a bubble bath drinking from a bottle of wine. On the ground floor was the tiny bistro where every night we ordered the same veal dish, heavy with wild mushrooms and cream.

Jack and I returned to Paris twelve years later. With maps in our hands, we raced through the streets to find that romantic hotel. Anxious to capture the feelings we had during our honeymoon, we planned to recreate our dining experience. But when we found the intersection and turned the familiar corner, we looked with disbelief. Our bistro had been turned into an Italian restaurant.

So this May when I heard from my daughter that their father, who had been 250 pounds when I married him, was down to 165 and had to endure weeks of chemo followed by a regimen of radiation, my heart broke. This man who loved to eat and cooked for our frequent dinner parties now needs a feeding tube.

When I was thinking of divorcing Jack, I struggled with the question of what is love. How can I say I love someone for years and then not love him? What's the difference between being in love and loving? Does the love change or do we change? If you truly love someone, is that love always there? What remains?

Jack called me in June, the day our son got engaged. His voice was weak and hoarse. A good and uncomplaining patient, he was confident about his doctors. I had trouble controlling an urge to sob, as I told him how sorry I was he had to go through this awful thing. His voice began to tremble. He cut the call short.

This July our daughter, who had been divorced for two years, married Dave Flannery, her high school boyfriend, at Southampton Town Hall. I called Jack to share the happy news. His voice sounded stronger and the treatments had shrunk the tumor sufficiently to enable him to take liquids and a little food by mouth.

"This illness is costing Judy too much money."

"What do you mean?"

"She drives me to the medical center and then goes shopping while I have my treatments."

Although they don't live together, Jack and Judy have been a couple for longer than the thirteen years my husband and I have been married. It helped me to get on with my life knowing that Jack had someone who loves to travel and play golf. Someone who lightens him up, something I couldn't do.

Our son's wedding is in late September. Initially we were trying to be optimistic about Jack being able to attend the celebration. But when he was operated on in August, they found more cancer and had to remove his stomach.

❖❖❖❖❖

The sand shifts, the sea swings in and out. What remains are the happy memories and the love I feel for Jack, the father of our daughter and son, a good man who loved me as best he could.

What remains is a silver cuff, a fixture on my left wrist. I bought it for myself at an estate sale and had it engraved *love Jack, May 2, 1984* for my 38th birthday. It had been years since Jack had made a grand gesture. Maybe it was a symbol of what I had hoped for.

From the bridge I spot two boats, one motoring in the other's wake until one steers to the right heading for dockage, while the other wends its way through the inlet into the ocean.

Treasures

I am happy to be home, back to my life that includes walking the bridge. So I fight a strong wind from the south and light rain that drops like tears on my face. It's thirty degrees cooler than Florida where the humidity matched the 92 degree temperature as lightning singed the sky. I was there with my daughter and son, and their spouses, to help free their father from a body that no longer served him.

Jack, my former husband, had been diagnosed with esophageal cancer in April. During his surgery that followed months of radiation and chemo, the doctors found that the cancer was more invasive then they had expected. They had to remove his stomach. He quickly developed a septic infection. After weeks in the intensive care unit he was released to another ward where he had a heart attack and was without oxygen for 15 minutes.

When his doctor called with the news, my daughter Melissa and her husband Dave packed their truck and left for Boynton Beach. My son Ashley, Lauren, his bride of three days and I flew to Florida the next day. Jack's girlfriend, Judy, picked us up at the airport and gave us the key to his house. She wouldn't be at the hospital the next day. She had said her good byes.

Jack had discouraged visitors when he was undergoing chemo and radiation. Ashley and Lauren decided to visit him the day before his operation on August 25th since it seemed unlikely that he would be at their nuptials a month away. Jack had insisted that the wedding go on as scheduled. Melissa and Dave, who had been married at a Justice of the Peace at the end of July, planned to spend time with Jack in the fall. I had spoken to Jack and sent him cards but I hesitated to visit because I didn't want to intrude on Judy's space. At the end I knew I had to go for myself and to be with my children. We all wished we had gone sooner.

Down a maze of corridors in the ICU we walked by opened doors with beds cocooned in white curtains. We passed room 207 because we didn't recognize the man in an upright position in the bed. Back tracking I noticed the gauze patch over the right eye where his glass eye had probably been removed, and I knew it was Jack, my former husband of 25 years. Our children remained outside the room to speak to the nurse who would

At his side I rubbed his chest that dwarfed his ancient face, gaunt and discolored where the tape held the rubber tube of the ventilator in his gaping mouth. Cupping his swollen hand in mine, kissing his forehead, I whispered words I needed to say conscious of the minty scent that masked the smell of a dying man. My son and daughter and their spouses squeezed into the cubicle and surrounded Jack's bed.

On Monday we waited for the neurologist's report. After hearing it, we were even more certain that the decision to disconnect the breathing tube that kept their father tethered to this life was the right thing to do. The merciful thing to do. Jack had been emphatic about his wishes. It was a blessing that his sister, brother, and Judy agreed. Ashley was proxy for his father's living will. I reassured him that his decision was a gift of love.

We arrived at the hospital on Tuesday at noon and spent the day waiting – waiting for the doctor, waiting for the morphine, waiting for the medication that inhibited Jack's breathing to allow the ventilator to breathe for him to finish so that he would have a chance to breathe on his own, waiting for the four rectangular monitor screens to go dark, waiting for the ventilator to be disconnected, waiting for the oxygen numbers on the fifth monitor to drop from 96 to 0, waiting for the end. At 10:15p.m. Melissa's hand was on her father's chest when she felt his last breath leave with his soul.

From Sunday to Thursday we stayed at Jack's house with aqua metal hurricane shutters in a small development built in the seventies. Jack met Judy while playing golf on Long Island. She had inherited her mother's house in Boynton Beach; he bought one around the corner from her. Although they traveled the world together, they never married and maintained separate residences for the fifteen years they lived year round in the sunshine state.

I slept on an air mattress in the second bedroom which had been converted to an office where the walls were decorated with golf posters from the 1995 US Open in Southampton, a photo of Jack shaking Arnold Palmer's hand, an antique putter. His golf clubs retired at the end of his desk next to cases of liquid nutrition and a stainless steel pole that held his feeding tube. In the corner was a small empty wine cooler.

It was strange being with my children and realizing that they, not me, were in charge. I took a backseat while my children both in their mid-40s, made the decisions which were theirs to make. As I was thinking what should be done next, they were doing it. I know that my daughter and my son are thoughtful, competent people but it was rewarding to watch them handle this heavy responsibility with intelligence, compassion and humor. One of them joked "Two Weddings and a Funeral". Dave ribbed Lauren, "How's the honeymoon going?" I was glad that Jack waited until after the weddings to die, so that our children had their supportive spouses at their sides.

I helped the kids by making phone calls to crematoriums and the New York State Teachers retirement system while Ashley got in touch with his father's lawyer and Melissa started to gather framed Christmas photos of her sons. She culled clothes from her father's closets and drawers for her oldest, who at 14 with his grandfather's broad chest and shoulders, wears a size 48 coat. We were glad to have Dave's truck. Lauren asked Ashley to pack his father's rocking chair hoping someday to rock their children in it. I took a plaid cashmere scarf and water repellent Tilley Hat, which is guaranteed for life.

It depressed me to think that one's life comes down to piling, bagging, and shredding. We had only a few days to go through Jack's things since we wouldn't be coming back.

Judy had told us not to be surprised where we might find things. I offered to look through pants' pockets and drawers for hidden treasures. I did find a one hundred dollar bill tucked in Jack's underwear and a roll of singles in his desk. His wallet and two rings were in the bathroom vanity. One was his high school ring from Mount Saint Joseph's in Baltimore and the other his gold ring from Villanova which he had lost and then found shoveling snow in our front yard one winter. The stone was missing, but Judy had it filled with gold.

Actually I was secretly looking for any evidence of our twenty-five years together, a picture of me or us, some memento. In a leather box among foreign coins and pins from his travels and golf trips, was his gold wedding band from 1967. On his wall among collages of pictures taken on cruises with Judy to Alaska, Asia, New

Zealand, Hawaii, Europe was a poster with red, green and black stripes on a white background that used to hang on a wall in our house. It was from a track exhibition where we watched Olympian Greta Waitz race, the summer we traded houses with a family in Norway. My Christmas card from last year and a get well card were in a short stack on his desk.

It had rained the day we left lifting the humidity. When we closed the door behind us we were greeted by a rainbow arching across the sky. I looked up and realized it was a double rainbow, one for Melissa and one for Ashley, the true treasures from my marriage to Jack.

Ponquogue Parade

As I walk the Ponquogue Bridge I notice the landscape colors of the barrier island have changed with the season. Cord grass has turned from deep green to shades of pale champagne to golden butterscotch to pecan blonde. The Spike grass's silvery hue is now cinnamon brown. Beach plum, Virginia Creeper, and poison ivy's foliage burn copper and fire engine red. Northern bayberry's leaves are gone, replaced by platinum berries. The display resembles a Clairol color chart.

I've been dying my hair since I was thirty. Grey strands arrived uninvited after my daughter was born. When I got tired of older women stopping me in the supermarket and suggesting that I color my hair, I had it dyed a medium brown Ever since then, I have spent hours in a beauty salon every three weeks for most of my life. I'm done with that time and money commitment. Next year I will be 70. I feel a need for a change which seems to happen every decade.

During my stay at home days in the 60's, I wore my salt and pepper hair in a long braid that worked along with jeans and a leotard. When I returned to work, I became a brunette and opted for a Jane Fonda style bob. I added midi-length skirts with beautiful silver buckled belts and imported French suede and leather boots to be voted the best dressed teacher at my job in the 70's This look was followed by a short Dorothy Hamill cut, red power suits for union meetings, as well as my favorite navy blue Ellen Tracy suit with large gold buttons and many other future donations to Dress for Success.

By the mid 80's I was beginning to realize that I couldn't control the world. I let my hair grow and became more of a red head. The unbraiding of my marriage began with my fortieth birthday. During that decade I cut off my hair and permed it. The tight wiry curls became symbolic of how fried I was. By the time I met my sweetheart Terry in my fifties my hair was just long enough for an elegant up do when we got married in 2001.

Last summer I went to a fashion show at Stone Creek Inn to benefit Camp Good Grief. I noticed an attractive woman around my age on the opposite side of the room. At the end of the afternoon I rushed over and admired her hair which was white with dark low lights. She told me that she had at done at a pricey salon in Southampton. The good news was the tri-color process only has to be touched up every three months. That was the clincher.

My new hairdresser filled my head with flat foil packages. In less an hour I had blonde mixed in with my darker hair, so that when my natural white color grows in there won't be a drastic contrast.

The lighter hair around my fair skinned face is softer and I think more flattering, but the fun part is I feel like a different person. People tell me I now look like Diane Keaton. I'll take it. To complete the look I need big glasses to run interference with my wrinkles and turtle necks to hide my crepey chicken skin.

With the beginning of the end for the Baby Boomer generation, I have thought about end of life arrangements. A good friend from college kicked a potentially fatal disease that required Zombie like blood transfusions. To while away hospital time she planned detailed funeral arrangements down to the music and menu. I was inspired.

One day I shared the plans I had in mind for my final requests with my children. I told them that I want to be cremated and that I really like the Jewish tradition of sitting Shiva as opposed to an impersonal funeral parlor. I guess it got a little complicated when I mentioned a processional on the Ponquogue Bridge, and began questioning whether the grandchildren would be old enough to play music, or maybe I should just stick to bagpipes. My son said, "You know Mom, you are not going to be there."

So I decided instead of a processional when I am dead, why not a Ponquogue Parade to mark my 70th birthday? I'll invite anyone I ever knew to walk across the bridge with me. Then we'll celebrate with champagne and cake at the Pavilion overlooking the ocean as I begin the next decade living with a vengeance and a new look.

I will also be autographing my book BRIDGE WALKER.

You are all invited.